V Bobbitt

NAHANT.

Its Merits as a Fashionable Summer Resort.

Among the places of fashionable Summer Resort there is none more worthy of the attention of parties projecting summer tours than Nahant, the primitive pasture ground of the Pilgrim cows, but now an Eden of hot weather comfort and luxury.

It is about ten miles from Boston, as the bird flies, on a promontory that defends one side of its harbor from the winter North-easters, and would be an island if it were not for the narrow beach (just wide enough for a fine road way), five miles long, which connects it with Linn.

It comprises five or six hundred acres, long ago, as intimated, a colonial pasture, but now the site of thirty or forty villas and cottages, all dreary and bleak enough in winter, but in the heated time a Paradise of coolness and sea-breezes. Twenty years ago Nahant was one of the places that we read of. Then its great stone hotel was in its glory, and the tide of Summer travel ebbed and flowed in that direction before Newport was heard of. But the hotel declined, and, of course, Belledom deserted it. Old Ocean surged, and stormed, and sighed among the rocky caves, but only a transient visitor came down to admire, to regret, and to leave before sunset. Progress, however, came along, and its enterprise has converted the stone fortress of the last generation into the nucleus or centre of a great establishment,

"THE NAHANT HOUSE,"

from which you may toss a biscuit into the Atlantic on three sides.

Walks and Talks.

SONG FROM A NORTHERN SHORE.

The cold, gray sunset over lonely seas,
The granite coast that frowns upon the sand,
Are all that recompense me for the breeze—
... breeze that bore her from the land!

—MISS MELINDA BROADSKIRT, who has already opened the subject of smoking and spitting upon ...

The Lounger listens for a... din to Sacramento.

Adventures of America

From
Daddie Reed's
Library

ADVENTURES OF AMERICA

1857—1900

A PICTORIAL RECORD FROM

HARPER'S WEEKLY

By

JOHN A. KOUWENHOVEN

HARPER & BROTHERS PUBLISHERS

New York and London

1938

ADVENTURES OF AMERICA, 1857-1900

Printed in the United States of America

IN REMEMBRANCE OF

MY FATHER

PREFACE

THIS book is an informal history of life in the United States during the latter half of the nineteenth century. The text is designed both to explain and interpret the pictures, as captions would do, and to provide as connected and interesting a survey of social history as possible.

The pictures have been chosen from *Harper's Weekly*, the most representative illustrated journal of the time. Begun in the panic year of 1857, the *Weekly* built up an enormous circulation during the Civil War. In April, 1865, the *North American Review* carried an article about it which said,

> "It has been one of the most powerful organs of public opinion. Its vast circulation, deservedly secured and maintained by the excellence of its illustrations of the scenes and events of the war, as well as by the spirit and tone of its editorials, has carried it far and wide. It has been read in city parlors, in the log-hut of the pioneer, by every camp-fire of our armies, in the wards of our hospitals, in the trenches before Petersburg, and in the ruins of Charleston. . . . Our historical societies and public libraries throughout the country should secure a complete set of the volumes of *Harper's Weekly*, for every year will add to their value as an illustrated record of the times."

This enviable position of editorial influence was maintained until, in the second decade of the present century, the Weekly succumbed to the competition of the Sunday newspaper supplements.

To us the triumph of the *Weekly* was its artists—men like Thomas Nast, Winslow Homer, C. A. Reinhart, E. A. Abbey, Frederick Remington, and their compeers, who perfected journalistic illustration. Up until the last years of the century their pictures were either drawn directly on, or transferred to, blocks of box-wood. Skilled engravers then cut away all the wooden surface not covered by lines of the drawing, and the printing was done from the resulting blocks. In order to accomplish this lengthy process speedily enough to issue the paper once a week, a large staff of engravers was employed. Full-page or double-page illustrations were divided into sections, each of which might be engraved by a different man; after which the small blocks were locked together in a form, from which the entire picture was printed as a unit. The pictures on pages 00 and 00, for example, show quite clearly the joints between the various component blocks.

As we look at the pictures in the old *Weekly*, we are apt to be struck with a feeling that they are distorted and unreal. They did not seem so to those who bought them at contemporary newsstands. They are not merely quaint survivals from the past, but also vivid evidence of the way our ancestors looked at the America in which they lived. If we could climb back through the years and see the very scenes which are pictured in this book, they would not look like that to us. But they did look so to Americans of those days. In 1867 Walt Whitman sent his mother a copy of the *Weekly* containing Nast's picture of Lincoln and a drummer boy which he claimed was "tip-top," and another American poet found inspiration in one of the pictures for a poem which every schoolboy knows (see No. 74).

It has been difficult to choose from the vast number of illustrations in the forty-four nineteenth-century volumes of the *Weekly*. Primarily I have chosen those which seem to contribute most to a panorama of American life from before the Civil War until after the War with Spain. In many cases I have had to omit excellent drawings. There are, for instance, literally dozens of delightful sketches of the skaters in Central Park, yet obviously I could use only one. On the other hand, it has been necessary to use some illustrations of no artistic value because their subjects seem important.

Other difficulties were presented by the editorial character of the *Weekly*. As a contemporary journal it often gave enormous publicity to events which time has covered with unimportance, and it neglected material which the doubtful omniscience of posterity has hailed as significant. I have tried to preserve some of the contemporary bias of the editors with a minimum of violence to our viewpoint of enlightened retrospect. In this connection we must remember that the *Weekly* was a New York publication and that its interests were therefore predominantly metropolitan. While recognizing that the life of other cities somewhat resembled that of New York, I have, nevertheless, attempted to minimize the paper's provincialism.

Though the book is primarily an informal sally into America's past adventures with living, it aims also to be accurate. Mistakes in fact and errors in judgment doubtless occur, and I should be held rigidly to account for them, not excused because the book is designed for the general reader instead of for the special student. Contrary to current belief, the general reader is entitled to just as accurate facts as the specialist, though not so many of them.

In writing the text I have availed myself largely of the material in the magazine, reinforced with the best recent historical research which is available. I am particularly indebted to the following: A. C. Cole, *The Irrepressible Conflict,* Macmillan, 1934, Allan Nevins, *The Emergence of Modern America,* Macmillan, 1932, and A. M. Schlesinger, *The Rise of the City,* Macmillan, 1933 (which are volumes VII, VIII, and X of *A History of American Life,* edited by A. M. Schlesinger and D. R. Fox); S. E. Morrison and H. S. Commager, *The Growth of the American Republic,* Oxford, 1930; V. L. Parrington, *Main Currents in American Thought,* volume III, Harcourt Brace, 1930; C. A. and Mary R. Beard, *The Rise of American Civilization,* Macmillan, 1933; Claude Bowers, *The Tragic Era,* Halcyon House, N. Y. [1929]; Walter Millis, *The Martial Spirit,* Houghton Mifflin, 1931; the files of the New York and Chicago newspapers, and several magazines; and to standard biographies of eminent men and women of the period. For invaluable criticism, much of which I fear did no good, and for typing the entire manuscript, I thank my wife.

Dorset, Vermont J. A. K.
1938

CONTENTS

PREFACE

PART ONE — A House Divided, 1857-1860

PART TWO — The Scourge of War, 1861-1865

PART THREE — A New Nation, 1866-1876

PART FOUR — The Stormy Present, 1877-1893

PART FIVE — The Progress of Our Arms, 1894-1900

INDEX

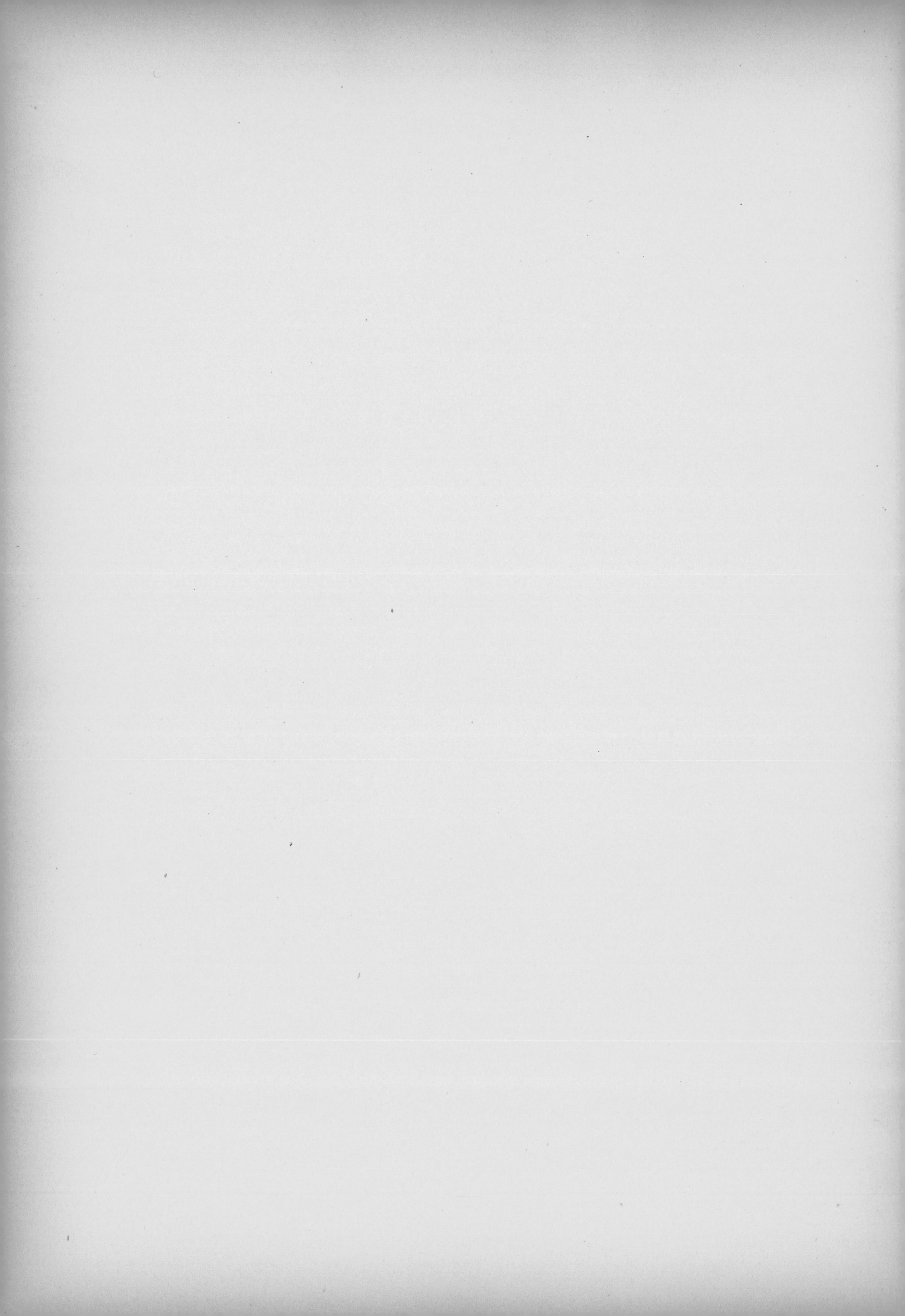

PART ONE

A House Divided

1857-1860

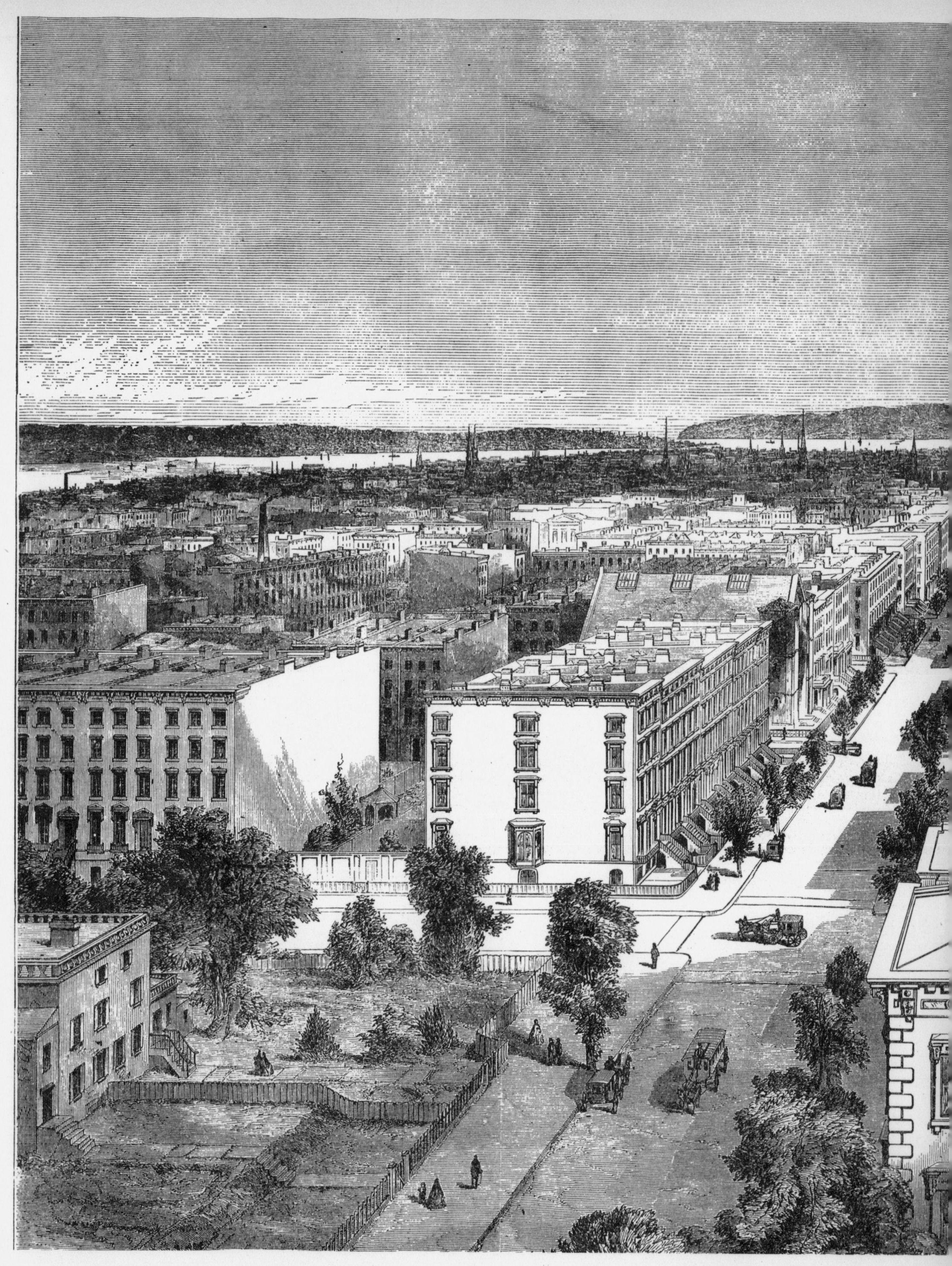

1. New York in 1857 was "a huge semi-barbarous metropolis . . . not well-governed nor ill-governed, but simply not governed at all—with filthy and unlighted streets—no practical or efficient security for either life or property—a police not worthy of the name—and expenses steadily and enormously increasing." (*Harper's Weekly,* April 11, 1857.) In other words it was the most thriving commercial city, the busiest port, in a great, gangling country which was growing up too fast. Its population increased by 300,000 in ten years. It was the sieve through which the bulk of European commodities and human beings passed into the fabulous new con-

Hitchcock

tinent; and, linked by railroads and waterways with the West, it served as broker for the products of the plains.

In the picture above we look down Fifth Avenue past the spire of the Brick Presbyterian Church (now about to be demolished—1938). Crossing the foreground is 36th Street. Just left of the church spire may be seen the cupola of the house on the north-west corner of 34th Street which was built by the notorious sarsaparilla enthusiast, Dr. Samuel P. Townsend, at a cost of $100,000, and was one of the city's show places. On the south-west corner of 34th, where the Empire State building now stands, lived William B. Astor.

William John Hennessy

2. To the port of New York came most of the immigrants who flocked to America at the average rate of 235,000 a year during the fifties. About half the city's population in 1860 was foreign-born. 200,000 immigrants from Ireland made it the largest Irish city in the world. More than 2,000 Italians were congested in one squalid section, whence itinerant peddlers sallied into the provinces, and where the less venturesome sold fruit and confections. The city's share of the nation's 150,000 Jews centered in the districts about Chatham Street and the Bowery, occupied chiefly with the clothing business. Some of the million and a quarter German immigrants settled, as they did in Cincinnati, St. Louis, Chicago, Milwaukee and Louisville, in a part of the city where they maintained the social institutions of the Fatherland at the same time that they embraced American customs and interests. Few of the Polish, French, Scandinavian, and English immigrants stayed in the great Atlantic ports, most of them moving on to the West.

3. In the first half-century there was no adequate shelter for these new arrivals. Americans persistently referred to them as emigrants, not immigrants, thus demonstrating that we thought in terms of their departure from Europe, rather than their arrival on our shores. As soon as they set foot on land they were exposed to runners, who charged exorbitant prices for aid with luggage; to scoundrels who sold them bogus railroad or boat tickets; and perhaps to less elaborate thieves, who simply robbed them by force. In 1855, however, the Commissioners of Emigration leased the famous old Castle Garden on the Battery, and changed it from an

A. R. Waud

amusement hall into a depot where the bewildered foreigner could find interpreters, guides, authorized ticket-agents, and an information bureau.

4. In such buildings as these lived the more fortunate poor of large American cities. By 1860 there were more than ten thousand tenement houses in New York. About a twentieth of the population of Boston and New York lived underground in damp, dark rooms among filth and vermin. When, in 1860, New York provided for a system of sanitary police to improve these conditions, the slum owners applied to Tammany for appointments as health inspectors and got them. The death rate in the city almost doubled that of London.

The tenements were firetraps. Ten people were killed in this one at No. 90 West 45th Street. Martin Redman and his family, who lived in one room behind the "Fancy Grocery" and liquor store which they ran, escaped unhurt; but the wives and children of Thomas Bennett and Andrew Wheelan, both of whom were employed in the Sixth Avenue Railroad Company's stables, were burned to ashes.

5. Broadway was already the most famous street in America. Here were the great stores, the finest hotels. The corner of Broadway and Fulton Street was the Times Square of the fifties, where every visitor gravitated to see the whirling activity of traffic, the great shops, and especially Barnum's Museum, that unprecedented

scramble of marvels and humbugs, to which such hordes of people came that Barnum had to devise some way to be rid of them. He disguised the exit, making it look like the entrance to another exhibit, and hung over it a sign which read: "To the Egress." Eager to get a look at this unheard-of monster, the yokels flocked out into the street.

Winslow Homer

6. The Broadway of Boston was Washington Street. Winslow Homer, one of the ablest American artists of the nineteenth century, did some of his most vigorous work for *Harper's Weekly.* Here he presents us with Washington Street on a spring day, the ladies in their finery promenading with their escorts, a child with the then favorite toy—a hoop to roll or toss, and a poor woman selling lilacs.

8. Governor Geary, of Kansas Territory, had no such elegant capital as the Governor of New Hampshire. In this six-room mansion at Lecompton he was faced with the turmoil of pro-slavery and anti-slavery rioting, which had resulted in the Ossawatomie raids in which one of John Brown's sons was killed and another driven insane by inhuman treatment. (See No. 221.)

7. Throughout New England there were small cities and large towns where an aristocracy of wealth, based largely on increased land values, controlled factories which manufactured shoes, machinery, textiles, and other products, the raw materials for which came chiefly from the West and the South. Here is Concord, New Hampshire's capital, where the Walkers, Bradleys, Rolfes, and Eastmans held their inherited land, while immigrants flooded into the factories at a rate which increased the population 150% in fifteen years.

9. Farther west in Utah Territory, however, Governor Brigham Young had built himself a desert commonwealth. With shrewd benevolence he led his Mormon followers in the creation of a fertile, thrifty agricultural community out of the arid Great Salt Lake valley. Irrigation canals, totaling about 1,000 miles in length, brought water from the surrounding mountains to the farms. Good roads, good schools, fine buildings, an admirable theatre, and a thriving church combined to make Salt Lake City a beautifully planned capital of almost 15,000 people. The picture shows the government-controlled Deseret Store where local products were sold, and the tithing house. The many-gabled building to the right of the store was the Lion House, where most of Young's wives lived. Farther to the right, with a cupola on top, was the house of Lady Young, the Governor's first wife, and her family. The group of buildings back of the tithing store was Heber C. Kimball's harem and home. The wall at the left of the picture surrounded the Mormon Temple block, and the stone marker, near the corner of the wall, was the point from which the first U. S. Survey of the Territory had started.

But the prosperity of Deseret, as the Mormons called their country, was responsible for its downfall. Non-Mormons came in to represent the Federal government, or to capitalize on the trade which grew up with the immigrants who traveled to the gold fields by way of Salt Lake. During the late fifties considerable furor was caused by the Mormon War, and the massacres which resulted from Young's attempt to repel the newly-appointed Federal Governor and his 1500 Federal troops. After a year of excitement, the Mormons agreed to respect the authority of the United States, and the affair blew over.

A. R. Waud

10. In homes like this, which belonged to Jefferson Davis of Mississippi, a landed aristocracy of slave-holding planters lived south of Mason and Dixon's line in luxurious leisure, holding patriarchal and polished sway over social and political life. Yet out of five or six million whites in the "black belt" of the South, there were less than four hundred thousand slave-owners, and only about two hundred and fifty thousand of these really profited from the plantation system. The whites who owned no slaves were divided into three main groups: small planters and professional men; a large number of tradesmen, skilled laborers, and farmers; and the poor whites, who lived in sloth and idleness in the back-country hills. Among the great planters there was a secure feeling that cotton was indispensable to the manufacturers of the North. "The North without us would be a motherless calf, bleating about, and die of mange and starvation," wrote the Senator from South Carolina in 1860. It was hard to realize that the South's combined cotton, tobacco, rice, hemp, and sugar harvest in 1850 had scarcely equalled in value the North's hay crop alone. All was not well in Dixie.

11. To Washington from each section of the straggling Union of states came Representatives and Senators to mold the course of national government. Politically, as well as socially, the southern states dominated the capital during the fifties, despite the greater wealth and larger population of the North.

Early in the fifties the split between North and South had seemed imminent, and the senator from Mississippi had suggested enlarging the cramped quarters of the capitol building with north and south wings which would symbolize the indivisibility of the sections. His name was Jefferson Davis.

But at the end of the decade the dome of the enlarged building was still ominously incomplete.

POLICE CONSTABLE (*to Boy*). "Now then, off with that Hoop, or I'll precious soon Help you!"
LADY (*who imagines the observation is addressed to her*). "What a Monster!" [*Lifts up the Crinoline, and hurries off.*

12. While sectionalism became increasingly bitter throughout the land, an even more absorbing topic of discussion was the new-fangled hoopskirt. Here is one of many cartoons in the *Weekly* which ridiculed the fashion, this one also poking fun at the police, who were an equally popular butt for satire. But the hoops, like the police, survived, and in 1859 the *Weekly* stated categorically that "Rightly or wrongly, the esthetic eye requires that the female figure shall be broader at the base than at any other point. . . . Certainly a woman without hoops, with garments clinging to her person, and exposing, in the wind, the contour of every limb, is neither gracefully nor delicately attired." (Feb. 12, 1859, p. 99.)

13. Miss Flora M'Flimsey of Madison Square had, as the most popular poem of the day informs us, Nothing to Wear, though her wardrobe was stuffed with such fashionable garments as these. The two ladies at the left are dressed for indoors; the one pulling on gloves of "pale yellow kid" wears brown silk, crossed with chequers of black satin, trimmed with black velvet and Maltese lace, while the other supports violet-colored terry velvet, trimmed with black velvet, black guipure, and Venetian lace. The ball dress is of white tulle illusion, figured with small sprigs worked in blue silk. Under the opera cloak (white cashmere trimmed with pink plush, figured with white spots) is a double-skirted dress of pink silk, each skirt being trimmed with three rows of white feather fringe.

Alfred Fredericks

14. May Day in New York was moving-day, as it had been since the days of the Dutch. The custom originally sprang from a city ordinance which required anyone who was going to move to do it by May 1st, in order that the city directory could be made up on schedule.

During the 'fifties it became so fashionable to move that some fine ladies were ashamed to have it known that they were remaining another year in the old house. We should probably think that the house servants, upon whom most of the labor of moving devolved, earned a full month's wages on May Day, inasmuch as their salaries ranged from as low as four dollars a month for a maid-of-all-work, to a top of sixteen dollars a month for the best cook.

15. The idea of living in the suburbs of the city and commuting to business was just beginning to attract the wealthier citizens. The war, of course, put a temporary stop to the building of such houses as this in Tarrytown, New York, which belonged to A. V. Stout, Esq.

16. Though comparatively few could manage to commute from a country home, "everybody," said the *Weekly*, "but a few editors and other slaves" got away for at least a short vacation during the summer. Many went by boat, like the hot and harried throng embarking above. Others, who went by railroad, had often to wait for hours on rural station platforms to make connections with the uncertain trains.

Winslow Homer

17. A favorite place for the young ladies of New York to take their parents was Cozzens Hotel at West Point, where, during the summer months, the cadets at the Military Academy gave a "hop" three times a week. In the summer of 1859 Winslow Homer went to draw this picture of one of the hops and expressed his gratitude for their courtesy to the members of the cadet committee of arrangements. Two of these cadets, who graduated in 1860, were brigadier generals when they met four years later as enemies at the Battle of Gettysburg. General Stephen D. Ramseur, of the Confederate forces, was later killed at Winchester, resisting Sheridan's attack; while General Wesley Merritt of the Union army survived and was in command of the first American troops to land in the Philippine Islands during the Spanish-American War. (See No. 247.)

Winslow Homer

18. Newport, Rhode Island, was the most fashionable of the sea-bathing resorts. Wealthy Southern planters and their families were the first to seek its cool breezes, but rich New Yorkers and others soon followed their example. Elaborate hotels and pretentious summer cottages sprang up along the shore. Along the beach mixed bathing in relatively cautious garments was, as Winslow Homer's picture shows, a merry new pastime. Clear evidence of the growing breach between North and South came when, toward the end of the decade, the Southerners began to boycott Northern resorts in favor of such popular Southern places as Old Point Comfort or Fauquier White Sulphur Springs.

19. August Belmont, head of a great banking house, husband of the "Great Commodore" Perry's daughter, and U. S. minister to the Netherlands from 1853 to 1857, was one of the social leaders at Newport. He could be seen driving on the beach in his low barouche which cost $5,000, behind four fiery thoroughbreds worth $25,000 apiece, exclusive of harness and other trappings worth $3,000, with two postilions selected "with special reference to their build and the size of their calves," whose livery was imported at $1,000 a suit.

Augustus Hoppin

Augustus Hoppin

20. Those who chose to avoid the elegance and formality of Newport and the great hotels at Saratoga (where $1,500,000 was spent annually), sought out places like the Mountain House in the Catskills, the smaller resorts along the shore, or one of the White Mountain hotels, which were reached by coaches like these.

21. Even if a real vacation was impossible, the city dweller could get out into the woods and fields for picnics. Near every large city there were favored picnic grounds like those across the river from New York at Hoboken's Elysian Fields, where Winslow Homer made this drawing.

22. But for the dwellers in the tenements there was no country except the parks. Perhaps the best-known park in America was Boston's Common, with its fountain and great elm. Down from the mansions of Beacon Hill, at the right of Homer's picture, came the children of the Brahmins to play with their hoops or feed the squirrels. But not all the children came from Beacon Hill.

Winslow Homer

Winslow Homer

W HOMER DEL

Winslow Homer

23. When Central Park in New York was opened in 1860, the *Weekly* hailed it as a "sylvan miracle, teeming with bowers of romantic loveliness and dripping fountains of clearest crystal."

With the coming of cold weather the ponds of the new park were packed with crowds of ten thousand skaters or more. It was all part of a contemporary burst of interest in sports, led by such writers as Holmes, Edward Everett, Bayard Taylor, and Thomas Wentworth Higginson whose enthusiasm for skating earned it the nickname of "Higginson's revival." In Boston large crowds went on special trains to skate at Jamaica Pond.

24. The first convention of baseball clubs was held in New York in 1857. Delegates from sixteen organizations met to establish uniform rules for the game. But even in 1859, when Brooklyn played Philadelphia at the Elysian Fields in Hoboken, the *Weekly* could only report vaguely that "Baseball differs from cricket, especially, in there being no wickets. The bat is held high in the air. When the ball has been struck the 'outs' try to catch it, in which case the striker is 'out'; or, if they cannot do this, to strike the striker with it when he is running, which likewise puts him out. Instead of wickets, there are at this game four or five marks called bases. . . ."

Notice that no gloves were worn.

25. These gentlemen are Freshmen and Sophomores (in top hats) at Harvard about to play football, a rough sport which usually ended in a free-for-all fight. Harvard, like most colleges of the period, was "simply a more advanced school for boys. . . . The professors are task-masters and police officers, the President is chief of the College police" (*Atlantic Monthly,* vol. xviii, p. 299). But there were stirrings of real intellectual achievement at Harvard and elsewhere. Science and history continued to gain ground against the classics. New colleges sprang up in abundance, particularly in the South, where an increasing desire was manifest to become independent of Northern culture.

Winslow Homer

26. The drive in Central Park appealed to Winslow Homer as a scene of fashionable diversion. More serious were the trotting-races, which drew huge crowds throughout the country. Flora Temple, foaled near Utica in 1845, sold as a four-year old for $13, and bought in 1858 by Mr. McDonald of Baltimore for $8000, trotted a mile in 2 minutes 19¾ seconds in 1859, a record unbeaten for eight years.

Winslow Homer

27. The American theater was actively patronized. Despite the financial panic of 1857, the manager of the New York Opera announced that the season of 1857-58 was the best ever. Stage versions of "Uncle Tom's Cabin," "Ten Nights in a Barroom," and "Rip Van Winkle" were ubiquitous. The ballet aroused enough interest for the *Weekly* to present this "perfectly reliable" likeness of Emma Livry, a sixteen-year-old French girl, who had Paris at her feet. The editors announced apologetically that they had to illustrate current events, even though "the ballet is an institution with which serious-minded persons have as little to do as possible."

28. To some of the men who had lost money on the stock market during the 1857 panic it seemed that the reduction in the cost of living was more than counterbalanced by their wives' lack of resistance to the bargain sales of Broadway merchants. The *Weekly* did not mention the men who had lost their jobs and whose wives could not afford to shop even for bargains.

Thomas Worth

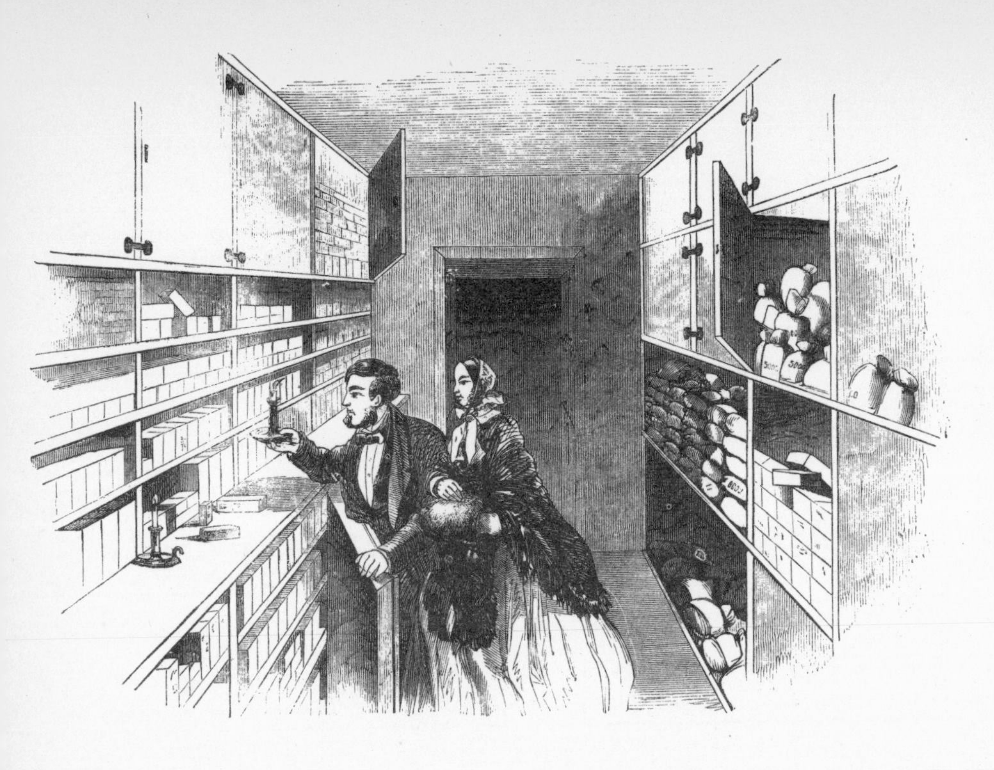

29. By the candle's light, a lady and gentleman inspect the vaults of the Sub-treasury in New York. They are looking at gold bricks worth $5492.35 each. Behind them are sacks of coin worth slightly less.

Many foreign notables had invested heavily in United States Government securities, and from these vaults went regular gold payments to several of the Saxe-Coburg-Gothas (whose relatives rule the British Empire), to the King of Naples' brother, the dramatist Scribe, Thomas Babington Macaulay, and the Count of Paris. Perhaps the Count was motivated by a desire to protect his investments, as well as a desire to learn the art of war, when he served as a Federal volunteer during the Civil War.

30. So rapidly had manufacturing, mining, and mill-work spread from the North Atlantic coast to the valley of the Ohio, that by 1860 the United States was no longer predominantly an agricultural country. The clothing industry profited by the aid of sewing-machines which could, for instance, complete a man's frock coat in two hours and thirty-eight minutes, which would have taken over sixteen hours by hand. The hoopskirt factory pictured here, supplied "healthy and lucrative employment" to about 1,000 girls and turned out as many as 90,000 hoopskirts per month. Into these 90,000 skirts went 150,000 yards of muslin, 100,000 feet of whalebone, 24,000 spools of cotton, 500,000 yards of tape (more than enough to stretch from New York to Boston), 225,000 yards of jute cord, 10,000 yards of haircloth, and 30 tons of steel. The owners proudly admitted that "smart girls" could easily make four dollars a week in their employ.

To Northern merchants and bankers, and to manufacturers like the owners of this plant, purchasers in the South owed two or three hundred millions of dollars by the end of the decade—a fact which partly explained the former's enthusiasm for preserving the Union.

W. S. & C. H. THOMSON'S SKIRT, MANUFACTORY.

31. Maine annually produced lumber valued at $5,000,000. The trees were cut in the forests on the upper regions of the Penobscot River, dragged over the snow to the banks of streams, and shot down in the spring on swollen waters to such cities as Bangor, where two hundred sawmills cut the logs into boards and planks.

32. Although industry was outstripping agriculture, the opening up of the fertile Western prairies and the beginnings of scientific fertilization increased the nation's crops. The large Western farms required different methods from the old New England acres, and machine reapers were in demand. Cyrus McCormick, originally of Virginia, had moved to Illinois, where several competing machines were manufactured. Reaper trials were held at many fairs. Our picture shows the trials at the Syracuse, N. Y., meeting of the United States Agricultural Society in 1857. Ninety-five different machines were tested. It was estimated that more than 20,000 of these machines were made in 1857 and sold at an average price of one hundred dollars.

Edwin Forbes

33. But old methods of agriculture persisted on many farms. Here we see a yoke of oxen hauling a load of corn. These powerful but leisurely beasts were only gradually replaced by the sprightlier horse. There were still as many oxen as horses in New England in 1860, and they remained even longer in the West. Mules were much used in the South, and experiments with camels on the prairies were successful though half-hearted.

34. In grain elevators like these at the Illinois Central Railroad depot in Chicago were stored the products of the prairies, awaiting shipment to the East. In spite of the poor crops of 1857 and 1858, the imports and exports of Chicago in the latter year equaled one quarter of the entire foreign trade of the United States. Linked by a growing network of railroads to many Eastern cities, Chicago had in thirty years become a city of 100,000 inhabitants, with horsecars, more than sixty hotels, and many fine buildings.

35. Though Chicago, with superior transportation facilities, was the greatest meat-packing center in the West by 1860, Cincinnati was an important rival. Hogs raised throughout the Ohio Valley were driven, or carried by boat or train, to Cincinnati, where 450,000 were slaughtered and distributed annually. Owing to the lack of refrigeration, all the meat-packing industry had to be carried on during the four cold months of the year.

36. In this fine Cincinnati mansion lived Nicholas Longworth, grandfather of the Speaker of the House who bore his name. Longworth was an eccentric millionaire who had gone to Cincinnati in 1803 as a young lawyer. As his first legal fee he accepted two copper stills, which he traded for thirty-three acres of land, which, as the city grew, came to be worth $2,000,000 to him. Having retired from law, he devoted his time to raising strawberries and to developing vineyards of Catawba grapes, from which he made a famous wine. Wine-growing became an important industry in Hamilton County especially.

37. In this Illinois house lived another able, though less wealthy, Western lawyer. It was a two-story frame house of eight rooms, its furniture abundant and of good quality, and supplied with an adequate assortment of books, pictures, statuettes, and "fine litter" generally.

At first it had been only one and a half stories high, and its exterior had boasted no carved cornices nor fancy moldings of any kind. As the lawyer's practice grew his wife demanded a more fitting residence, but he did not fancy the consequent presence of hammering and sawing carpenters, and was content with things as they were.

Finally, while he was away from home for several days, the lady called in the carpenters to add a story to the house and "put on some gingerbread." Returning home, the lawyer beheld the transformation and went about asking his old neighbors whose grand house had replaced his during his absence, and if they knew where Abraham Lincoln lived now.

38. The decade of the 'fifties was the great era of the American merchant marine. The tonnage of our ocean traffic almost doubled in ten years, and most of it was under sail. But the most spectacular achievement of the period was the introduction of great transatlantic steamships. The United States Government subsidized the Collins Line, which gave strong competition to the British Cunard. Americans in general agreed with the passenger on the S.S. *Adriatic* after its nine-day crossing, who was proud of the triumphs of his countrymen "over haughty Britannia."

M. Nevin

Largest and grandest of these ships was Britain's illfated *Great Eastern*, shown coming into New York Harbor through the Narrows on her first crossing, June 17-28, 1860. She was about 690 feet long, weighing 25,000 tons, and cost about $3,000,000. On her maiden voyage forty-three passengers rattled about in accommodations for four thousand. That was prophetic; for the great seamonster was never a success except for laying ocean telegraph cables. Her first stay in New York was so badly managed, as far as the eager crowds of visitors were concerned, that America sourly recommended a return to the original name of *Leviathan*, "since her owners were destined to blubber."

39. On August 16, 1858, Queen Victoria of England and President Buchanan of the United States exchanged greetings over the first Atlantic telegraph cable. Cyrus Field, Peter Cooper, Samuel F. B. Morse, and others had acquired subsidies from the British and United States Governments, and with the aid of the American ships *Niagara* and *Susquehanna*, and the British *Leopard* and *Agamemnon*, the cable was laid after several heart-breakingly unsuccessful attempts. Great was the rejoicing both here and abroad. Banquets, celebrations, and parades like this were held in every city of the land. Tiffany and Co., then at 550 Broadway, advertised four-inch lengths of the left-over cable, neatly mounted, at fifty cents each. A Broadway family chemist produced "Atlantic Cable Bouquet," a perfume "distilled from ocean spray and fragrant flowers," which he dedicated to Cyrus Field. Meanwhile the cable's faulty insulation rendered the messages fainter and fainter, until on September 4th they ceased entirely. It was eight years before a successful cable was laid, by the *Great Eastern.*

40. The demand for rapid communication naturally renewed interest in aeronautics. Men clung stubbornly to the notion that a balloon could be steered. Professor Wise, of Lancaster, Pennsylvania, managed to drift 1,150 miles from St. Louis to Jefferson County, New York, in June, 1859, without actually dying. Inspired by such an achievement, a young man named Carlincourt Lowe proposed a transatlantic flight. With the financial backing of several worthy citizens, he devised this airship. From the wicker basket, in which the aeronauts were to dwell, was suspended a small side-wheeler steamboat, powered by a four horse-power coal engine, which would carry them if the balloon went flabby in mid-ocean. The wheel-like propeller was not designed to move the ship forward, but only up and down. The protuberance at the other end is not a fog-horn, but one of those unsuspectedly futile rudders. Professor Lowe cautiously planned to take with him passports for all the European countries, just in case he should miss Spain, but a series of misfortunes and the advent of Civil War prevented his leaving New York. Lowe subsequently did pioneer work with observation balloons for the Union army.

41. In the year 1858 alone forty-seven steamboats on Western rivers sank, nineteen burned up, and nine exploded. Some were wholly inadequate craft, but many were large, luxurious vessels like the *Pacific*, a wood-burning side-wheeler, which plied between Louisville and New Orleans. She was 300 feet long, had staterooms for 120 passengers, a "semi-Gothic and Corinthian" cabin, a barber-shop, and a bathroom. It was such a ship as this which Mark Twain piloted in his early days.

42. Since 1850 six mules had hauled a heavy United States mail-coach, guarded by eight armed men, between Independence, Missouri, and Santa Fé, and the Mormons managed a similar service between St. Joseph and Salt Lake City. But it was not until 1858 that the mails reached California overland. In that year, Butterfield's Overland Mail, subsidized by the Government, began its semi-weekly service between St. Louis and San Francisco. Four horses, changed every ten or fifteen miles, pulled the six-passenger coaches day and night over the 2,729-mile route through plains, deserts, and mountains, in less than twenty-four days. The route swung far south, through the uninhabited regions of Texas, where there was no water for seventy-five miles at a time; on to Tucson through wild, mountainous country; then north through the Sierra Nevadas, and finally to San Francisco. The picture shows the Overland Mail coach leaving Butterfield's San Francisco headquarters on its very first trip.

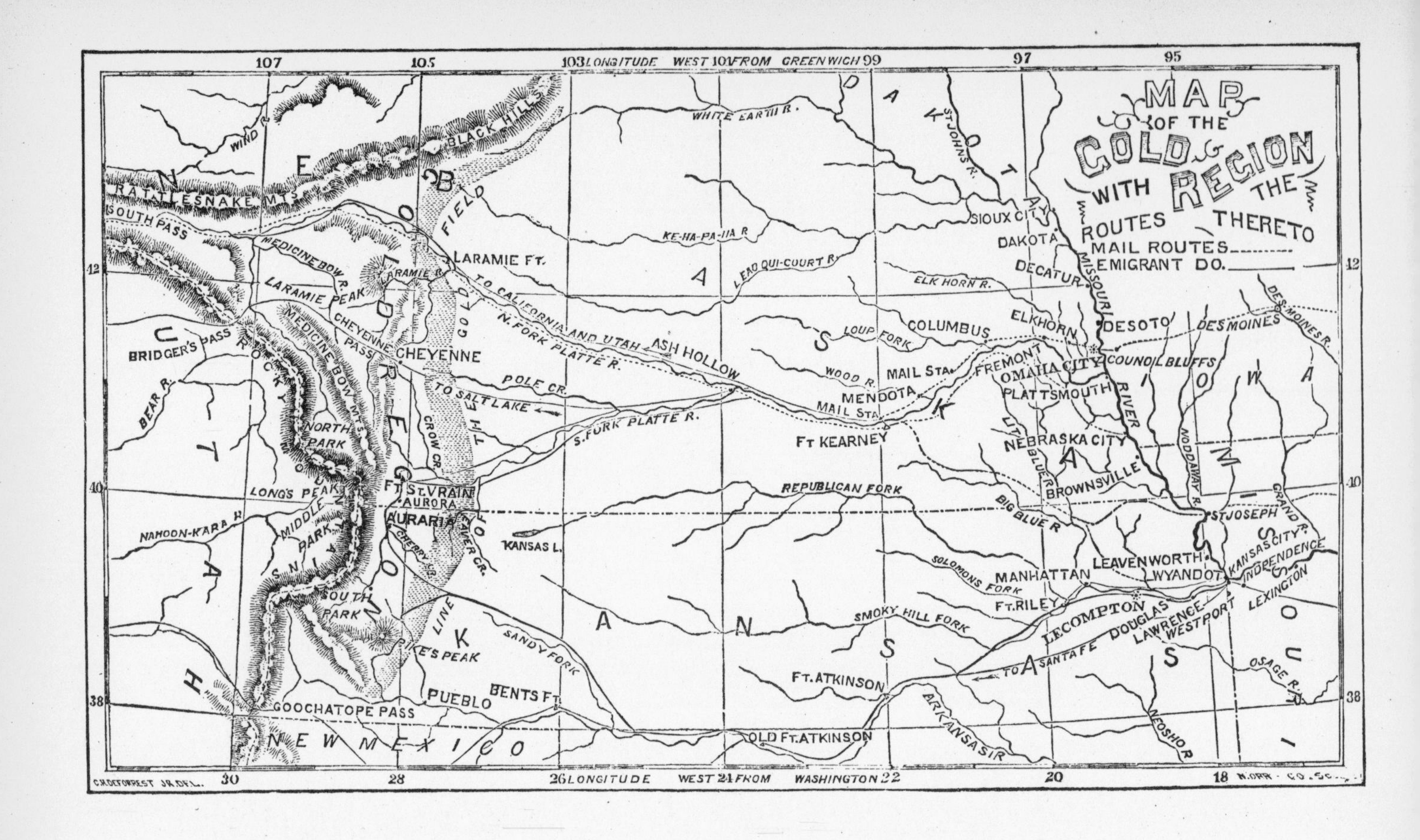

43. The discovery of gold near Pike's Peak in 1859 drew thousands of prospectors from California and the border settlements. The *Weekly* published this map for the benefit of those who rumbled overland in wagons bearing the crudely-lettered slogan, "Pike's Peak or Bust." The shortest route to the mines from Kansas City (lower right) was 740 miles. Boats or trains took the gold-seeker up the Missouri to St. Joseph, from which a weekly stage-coach would carry him, for fifty dollars, the 337 miles to Fort Kearney (center of map). There he had to wait for the weekly coach to Fort Laramie in the gold region. A mining outfit with tools and provisions for six months cost from fifty to sixty dollars.

Great Eastern Docks.
The Point of Embarkation.

44. As the gold excitement died down, the country turned to entertaining and gaping at two groups of distinguished foreign guests. Most exciting was the visit of H.R.H. Albert Edward, Prince of Wales, and suite. The following items from the index of the *Weekly* for 1860 are samples of the journalistic debauch which resulted: "The Prince and his dog; the Prince and the ladies; the Prince at West Point (and everywhere else he went); the Prince blushes; the Prince cannot hunt buffalo; the Prince dances twenty-two times; the Prince eats; the Prince falls down; the Prince lays a cornerstone; the Prince reads the papers; will the Prince marry an American?"

This popular young guest, sole object of conversation "in ninety-five out of a hundred drawing-rooms," sailed for England from Portland Harbor amid elaborate ceremonies. The long dock, from which he embarked, had been built to receive the *Great Eastern*, which subsequently changed its plans and went to New York.

Alfred Fredericks

45. Our other visitors were the Japanese ambassadors—first representatives of their empire to visit a Western nation. Thanks to the ingenious Commodore Perry, we had hoodwinked the Shogunate into a commercial treaty in 1854. By 1860 a new treaty was advisable, and we sent a naval vessel to bring to Washington the bewildered but magnificently unruffled diplomats shown above. "They are the queerest people to deal with," lamented President Buchanan; "there's no getting anything out of them, they're so close about everything."

46. Our interest in the trade of the Orient was a symptom of the same empire-ailment which prompted the frequent schemes for acquiring Cuba. Besides the ferment of the Cuban patriot groups in New York, there was agitation in the South for increasing slave territory. Senator John Slidell introduced a bill in January, 1859, which proposed appropriating $30,000,000 to buy Cuba from Spain, but no action was taken.

Augustus Hoppin

47. Northern Abolitionists were not only opposed to an increase of slave territory, but strove to free slaves wherever they existed. Some daring Northerners tripped through the South, inciting slaves to make a getaway *via* the various "underground railroads." Southerners probably lost over a thousand slaves a year by such means.

To defend their property and to check any possible uprising of the blacks, Southerners unhesitatingly resorted to lynching for anyone, white or black, who caused trouble. In the Kentucky lynching illustrated here, an unexcited crowd deliberately fastened a beam out from the second story of the courthouse, tied one end of a rope about the beam and the other about the victim's neck, and threw him out of the window.

48. Then, in the night of October 16, 1859, John Brown of Kansas marched his army of thirteen whites and five negroes into Harper's Ferry, seized the Federal arsenal shown at the far end of the railroad bridge, and set about liberating the slaves on near-by plantations. The militia and the marines under Col. Robert E. Lee subdued the small band, and Brown was tried and hanged. The Weekly passed over the event as "merely the work of a half-crazed white" which "will have cost the Republicans many thousand votes" in the fall election. But the South was panicky; even the non-slaveholder now definitely regarded negro equality as a vivid menace to his safety, with the result that he, like the planter, would fight to preserve slavery.

49. In February, 1858, Emerson wrote in his Journal, "It is impossible to be a gentleman and not be an Abolitionist." But conservative Northern opinion frowned severely on the activities of Abolitionist agitators. When William Lloyd Garrison tried to hold a John Brown anniversary meeting in Tremont Temple, Boston, he and his cohorts were thrown out bodily by the citizens, who subsequently held a meeting which resolved that Brown's was a "nefarious enterprise," and humbly asked their Virginia brothers to help preserve a Union so important "to the interest of commerce, manufactures, and agriculture."

50. During the spring of 1860, candidates for the Presidency were chosen by four parties. The regular Democrats chose Douglas; the Southern Democrats put up Breckinridge on a platform of slavery extension and annexation of Cuba; the Union party, on a platform which ignored slavery, nominated Bell; and the Republicans, putting aside their actual leader, Seward, fixed upon one of those whose "obscurity protected them

from hostile combinations." By October some of the obscurity was dispelled, and the demonstration in New York which is pictured here was typical of the Union enthusiasm which Lincoln aroused throughout the North and West. But the people of the South were openly proclaiming their unwillingness to submit to a purely Northern administration.

PART TWO

The Scourge of War

1861-1865

51. With considerably less than half the popular vote, and with scarcely a vote from south of Mason and Dixon's line, Abraham Lincoln carried all the free states and received a large majority in the electoral college. South Carolina promptly seceded from the Union, followed by Georgia, Alabama, Florida, Mississippi, Louisiana, and Texas. Early in February, 1861, delegates from these states met at Montgomery, Alabama, and formed the Confederate States of America. Jefferson Davis, who had argued against secession in Mississippi, was elected president. His inauguration, shown here, took place at Montgomery shortly before Lincoln's at Washington. Within a few weeks Virginia, Tennessee, Arkansas, and North Carolina also seceded. But there was considerable Union sentiment among the people of these eleven states, and it was soon demonstrated to Davis that he would "have to sprinkle blood in the faces of the people of Alabama" or Alabama would "be out of the Confederacy in ten days."

52. On April 12, 1861, blood-sprinkling was attempted. Edmund Ruffin, seventy-five-year-old planter, editor, and patron of agricultural progress, fired the first gun against Major Anderson's garrison in Fort Sumter. After a siege in which no one was killed, Anderson surrendered to the Charleston militia on the 13th, and on the 15th Lincoln issued a call for 75,000 volunteers. The Civil War had begun.

If, said the *Weekly*, "the war be not brought to a speedy close . . . it will be the fault of Abraham Lincoln." Baltimore and Richmond should be seized while St. Louis, Louisville, and Memphis were taken, and the Mississippi River controlled. This "will probably take all summer," and then the Northern armies could move against the rebels of the Gulf States.

The fiction serial running in the *Weekly* at this time was Charles Dickens' *Great Expectations*.

53. As the startled North watched soldiers and supplies sailing from its ports, it realized that war was no longer merely a threat. It was an exhilarating and terrifying reality to those who watched the loading of the *Atlantic* and the *Baltic*, about to sail from New York under sealed orders.

54. There was cheering from thousands of throats as the Seventh Regiment of the New York National Guard marched down Broadway beneath waving flags. Thomas Nast was on hand with his pencil and made this sketch. It later served as the basis of his large oil painting which hangs in the Seventh's armory.

And amid the shouting and the blowing of trumpets could be faintly heard the snapping of the American Peace Society's backbone as it protested that it did not "lend the slightest countenance to rebellion."

Thomas Nast

55. Typical of the impromptu volunteers who rallied to the excitement of battle were the "roughs" who made up Colonel Wilson's Zouaves. "Boys," the colonel had said, "you want to come with me, eh! Well, if you do, three-fourths of you will be in your graves in three weeks!"

"Bravo! Good! Good!" was the unanimous reply of the totally untrained and undisciplined gang.

Six months later they were attacked by the Confederates near Fort Pickens, and would have been annihilated had not three companies of regulars come to their defense. "The volunteers were badly managed, and Colonel Wilson is very much censured for the inefficiency and want of skill displayed in the action. He did not arrive at the scene of action until all was over." Ten of his men were killed, sixteen wounded, nine taken prisoner. War wasn't proving to be an amusing game for mere adventurers.

56. Out in Dubuque, Iowa, volunteers were embarking for the journey down the Missouri to Cairo. From the Middle-Western and frontier states, and from the territories came men familiar with firearms in their battles with the Indians, who were to supply much-needed strength to the Northern army. It was to be an army of Westerners under Sherman which decided the conflict.

Theodore R. Davis

57. Here is a Confederate transport barge on the James River canal. The canal was as important for the movement of troops as it was later to be in the economic recovery of the South (see No. 102). President Davis' first call for 100,000 troops was soon followed by others for 400,000 more, and within a year half the eligible male population had enlisted to defend the Confederacy. The best available estimates show that the number of men eligible for military service in the South somewhat exceeded 900,000, while the North had more than 4,000,000. At no time during the war did either side have as many as half these men under arms, but the enthusiasm of the first year brought eager volunteers.

The Lager Bier Wagon

PUTTING UP TELEGRAPH WIRES

CARRYING MILITARY STORES TO CAMP

58. Meanwhile both the Union and Confederate commissary departments, hurriedly attempting to meet the problem of feeding the soldiers, were buying wagons, mules, and supplies. Here we see a lager beer wagon, probably on its way to one of the many regiments of German immigrants; a wagon train carrying salt beef and other food. In the third picture we see men of the signal department putting up one of the military telegraphs which proved so valuable, not only to the army, but also to the newspaper men who, during the war, developed the fundamental technique of modern news-reporting.

Winslow Homer

59. Throughout the land factories were engaged in the manufacture of ammunition. Winslow Homer's picture shows the filling of cartridges at the Watertown, Massachusetts, arsenal. Three hundred were employed there — men to insert the powder by means of small ladles and funnels, and women to insert the bullets.

60. The West Point Foundry at Cold Spring, New York, gave up such peaceful manufacturing as machinery for the Jersey City waterworks, and turned to the production of twenty-five guns and seven thousand projectiles a week.

61. One of the largest factors in the ultimate victory of the North was its sea power. The sloop-of-war *Brooklyn*, 2,000 tons, carrying fourteen guns, was one of the best fighting ships available at the beginning of the war. It was with such vessels and their successors that the Federal navy ultimately established its blockade of Confederate ports.

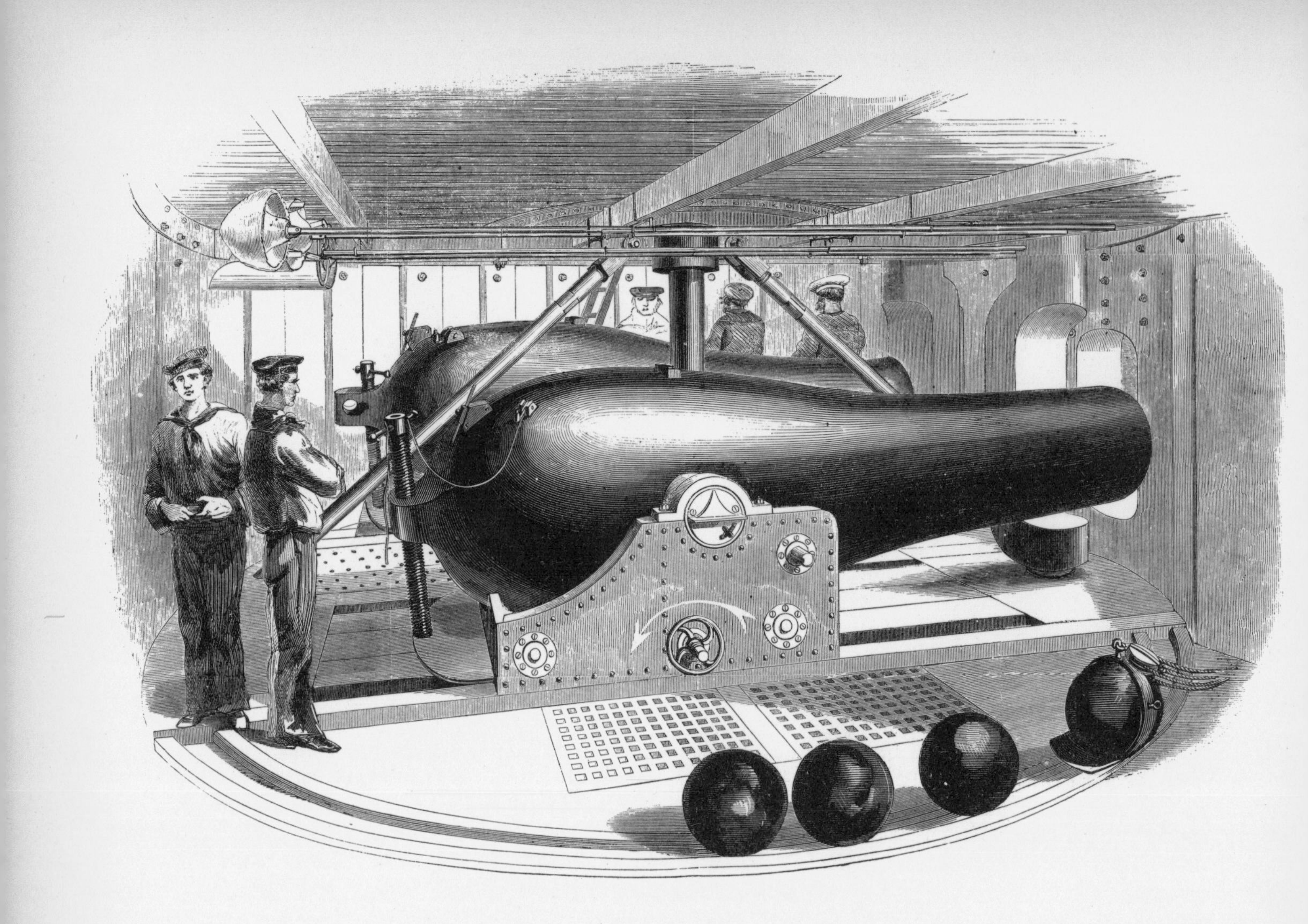

62. This picture of the turret on the United States ironclad *Passaic*, was inspected and pronounced accurate by its designer, Captain John Ericsson. This turret, called "the greatest engineering achievement of the time," contained twin Dahlgren 15-inch guns weighing 42,000 pounds each; yet it revolved easily without benefit of ball-bearings. To the left of the muzzle of the nearest gun may be seen the porthole-stopper, a heavy iron shield which could be swung around to close the porthole between shots, thus excluding enemy fire. In the foreground we see the 425-pound balls which were handled by an arrangement of pulleys and a sling.

Generally speaking, the Federal government was slow to adopt improvements in ordnance. The debate on the merits of muzzle-loading rifles *vs.* breech-loaders was not decided in favor of the latter until the war was almost over. But Ericsson's work with ironclads like the *Monitor* and the *Passaic* found instant favor.

Theodore R. Davis

63. In contrast with fighting ships like the *Brooklyn* and the *Passaic*, the first regular Confederate man-of-war was the *Lady Davis*, a little steamer armed with two boat-howitzers. Throughout the war, Southern naval operations were almost entirely confined to blockade-running and privateering, both of which were profitable enough to attract British capital and even the secret assistance of some Northern merchants.

MAKING GUN CARRIAGES
at the RICHMOND ARMORY

64. Following secession, the Confederates took over many Federal forts and arsenals within their territory. But the munitions thus acquired were not sufficient, and a number of munitions and powder factories were developed throughout the South. Here we have a sketch of the famous Tredegar works at Richmond, where gun-carriages are being made by hand.

65. There was comparatively little hand-to-hand fighting during the war, most of the battles being fought by infantry drawn up in opposing lines, the attacking force advancing slowly, halting to fire, until one side or the other gave ground. Sometimes, however, the double-quick advance was used, ending in bayonet fighting like that shown in Homer's picture. A soldier at the front thus described such fighting: "Men were bayoneted,

Winslow Homer

knocked down with the butts of muskets, and even fists were used in default of better weapons in that deadly strife. Officers used their dress swords, which they had hitherto considered as mere playthings for the parade, to hack down a troublesome enemy. . . . Men begged for more cartridges as they would for bread" (*Harper's Monthly,* October, 1864).

Winslow Homer

66. Homer also drew this picture of a sharpshooter on picket duty. According to the same soldier who described bayonet fighting on the previous page, "Sharpshooters play an important part in the operations of the army. Hiding themselves in a good position, they soon build a little pit, digging with a bayonet and tin cup. . . . Nothing short of an actual attack in force will dislodge [them]. . . . The enemy also have efficient sharpshooters who climb high trees and with their long-range rifles soon make themselves felt in our camp."

67. Aside from the regular armies there were guerilla bands in the West, who terrorized the countryside with their raids. Quantrell and the brilliant Southern cavalry officer, John Morgan, were known to North-

Thomas Nast

erners as the most daring guerilla leaders. Morgan's famous Kentucky raid was reported to have destroyed two million dollars' worth of property. Nast's picture gives his idea of Morgan's activities and proved an effective bit of anti-Confederate propaganda.

68. Of greater historical accuracy is Nast's drawing of a scene behind the lines during a battle. The reserves are lined up, waiting to be called into action. While they wait, they can watch the wounded being brought to the improvised hospital (at left) in front of which the surgeon is operating. On the table is a bottle of whis-

Thomas Nast

key, the only anaesthetic available, and scattered about on the ground are amputated arms and legs.

Such field hospitals as this were supplemented by two hundred and thirty general army hospitals, where many of the patients were victims of smallpox and camp fever. Of the more than 300,000 deaths in the Union army only a third were caused by wounds. Disease accounted for the rest.

69. Faced with the horrors of wounds and disease, often having little conception of why they were supposed to be fighting, numbers of men on both sides were demoralized. More than 200,000 Confederates deserted during the war; at the start of the second winter's campaigns over 100,000 were absent without leave from the Northern armies, and that number was increased by about 5,000 monthly for the war's duration. To combat this drain on man power, stern measures were adopted. The accompanying scene of a coward being drummed out of Union ranks was a common one, and military executions were almost as frequent.

70. While Walt Whitman was courageously nursing the wounded and mangled in Washington, other American authors were actively engaged in war. Among them was Major-General Lew Wallace, later the author of *Ben Hur: a Tale of the Christ*, who proved himself an able disciplinarian during his command at Memphis. In addition to deserters the army was cursed with men who used their weapons and uniforms to rob non-combatants. Four of Wallace's men were caught stealing half an ox. As punishment, Wallace ordered them to carry it on their shoulders around a tree all day in hour shifts; the next day they had to fan the carcass to keep flies off; and on the third day they buried it with elaborate funeral ceremonies.

71. This bearded officer was the hero of one of the first significant Union victories, the capture of Fort Donelson. He had served in the Mexican War, and been subsequently stationed in northern California. While there in 1854, he had resigned from the army to avoid court-martial for chronic drunkenness, and had later arrived in New York without a penny to his name. The man who lent him money then was Captain Simon B. Buckner, who, as General Simon B. Buckner, was one of the 15,000 Confederate prisoners taken at Fort Donelson.

Our officer later trimmed his beard, became General-in-Chief of the Union army, served two terms as President of the United States, and received among the last callers at his death-bed his old friend, Simon B. Buckner.

72. After Fort Donelson our officer (whose name, of course, was Ulysses S. Grant) had a very narrow escape at Shiloh, which almost ruined his career. Then came the siege of Vicksburg.

This strongly fortified town stood on a loop of the Mississippi, and Grant's first scheme was to dig the canal (shown here) to deflect and straighten the river, isolate the city, and permit Northern ships to descend to the Gulf. The canal was not dug deep enough. Nothing happened when the levee was cut, even though Grant had a stern-wheel steamboat fastened in place and tried to paddle the water in. By this time the season of high water had passed and the attempt was abandoned. A subsequent scheme involving Admiral Porter's advance with a fleet of gunboats through tortuous, tangled, and hitherto impervious bayous and creeks almost succeeded, but was forced to retreat under fire of Confederate sharpshooters. Amid these herculean difficulties Grant lost his false teeth.

Success finally came by marching his troops for frightful miles through swampy jungles and by running Porter's ships past the Confederate batteries. After months of hammering, Grant took the city on July 4, 1863.

Theodore R. Davis

73. In contrast with Grant's relentless driving tactics and the circumspection of McClellan were the brilliant maneuvers of Southern officers like Lee, Jackson, and J. E. B. Stuart. The accompanying illustration shows Stuart's cavalry on their dashing raid into Pennsylvania in October, 1862. Two thousand strong they rode up

A. R. Waud

to the west of McClellan's Army of the Potomac, crossed north of it through Chambersburg, and cut back into Virginia on the east, all without the loss of a dozen men. En route they captured large quantities of clothing, boots, and arms, and about five hundred horses.

Sol Eytinge

74. It was this picture of General Phil Sheridan's ride to the front, drawn by Sol Eytinge, which gave Thomas Buchanan Read the inspiration for his poem beginning:

> Up from the South at break of day,
> Bringing to Winchester fresh dismay. . . .

Sheridan was not a first-rate commander, but his theatrical performances as a cavalryman were grist to the schoolboy orators' mill, and Read's poem has won him almost legendary fame, while abler leaders on both sides have been all but forgotten.

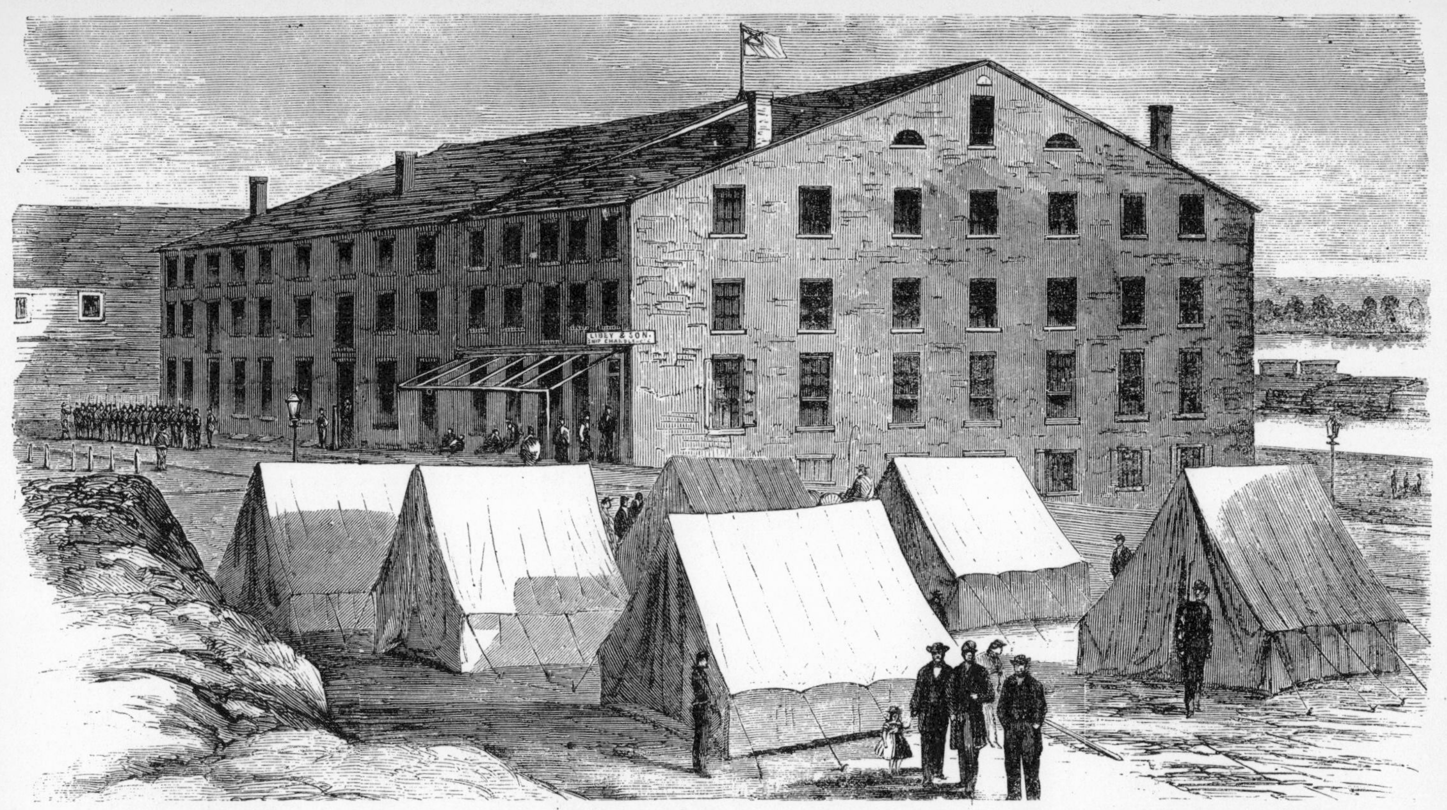

Capt. H. E. Wrigley, Topographical Engineers

75. Vast numbers of prisoners were taken by both sides, particularly by the Confederates after victories like Bull Run and Fredericksburg, and the horrors of military prison life were typified by the names of Andersonville and Libby (as it is incorrectly spelled). The latter was the warehouse of Libey and Son, ship chandlers in Richmond. Throughout the war and long afterward stories of brutality and gruesome agony centered about these prisons and prison camps, and were eagerly used in the North to fan the flames of sectional hate. Suffering there certainly was, but it must be remembered that the Confederate armies were starving and underfed during the period when the prisoners at Libey were abused, and that the Northern prisons, which could afford their inmates better treatment, reduced their rations to Southern levels in retaliation.

76. Behind the lines there was a public eager for news. Reporters and staff artists of the various journals followed the army into battle. This picture of Stonewall Jackson at his headquarters was a scoop for the *Weekly.*

The *London Illustrated News* had the artist Vizetelly stationed with the Confederate troops, and he drew this picture. The ship on which it was being carried to England was caught running the Union blockade at Charleston, and the *Weekly* somehow got the drawing from the Navy Department. Generally, however, Northern journals had little to offer about Southern life except sensational and unsubstantiated propaganda.

Henry Vizetelly

Winslow Homer

77. Most of the women of the country, North and South, turned courageously to the tasks left by the men who had gone to fight. There were clothes to be sent to the army, bandages to be rolled, and countless sacrifices to be made ir the household budgets. Many Southern women volunteered for munitions-making, and some courageously served as spies.

A. R. Waud

78. The war gave impetus to the employment of women in many positions. It was the working man who went to fight, and his wife or sister frequently took his place at the loom or the desk. Meanwhile, thousands of women poured into Washington to visit the wounded or to seek work, many with no funds. A great number of these became camp-followers, while others made themselves sufficiently attractive to politicians to be given clerkships in various government offices. The *Weekly* made no reference to the manner in which many of these clerks at the Treasury Department got their jobs.

79. Also in Washington was Mrs. Lincoln, who, desirous of impressing the hostile society of the capital, set an example of self-indulgent extravagance to the nation. This picture, drawn from a photograph by Brady, shows her in one of the gowns she bought on a trip to New York. Without her husband's knowledge she ran up a debt for clothes which could not nearly have been paid by his salary for an entire year as President.

80. Outdoing Mrs. Lincoln in vulgar show were the wives of the war-profiteers. Army contractors and speculators were "at a banquet of abundance and delight," and this cartoon of a contractor's wife is no exaggeration of the facts. To satisfy the wives of the profiteers the imports of luxuries rose to colossal sums. Women powdered their hair with gold or silver dust at fifteen dollars a dusting, and dined with their husbands at Delmonico's for a price per meal that would have fed a family for months.

81. Meanwhile the war was leading inevitably to the liberation of the slaves in the South, and it was already plain that these freedmen would raise serious social problems. Totally dependent upon their masters' care, absolutely uneducated, and never having known responsibility, their behavior was often childlike or pathetically bewildered. In the mansion of Robert W. Barnwell at Beaufort, North Carolina, the former slaves of the Confederate leader held carefree jubilation without a thought for the future.

82. Though the mass of slaves stuck loyally by their masters even after news of Lincoln's Emancipation Proclamation reached them, thousands seized opportunities to escape into Northern states; and a steady stream of contrabands, as they were called, struggled into Federal army camps, where they threw themselves upon the government's bounty.

83. Sentimental enthusiasm for notions of the brotherhood of man found frequent and sometimes elegant expression in the North. Early in 1862 a forty-year-old law decreeing that the slave trade was piracy was enforced for the first time when Nathaniel Gordon, a slave-trader, was hung.

But there was not a hearty welcome awaiting the freedmen from the South. A good deal was said about their stealing "the work and bread of the honest Irish and Germans," and, despite the efforts of a few leaders, they were almost universally denied any social or political rights.

84. Finding diplomacy difficult in midsummer Washington, Secretary of State Seward took the foreign ministers on a tour of our watering-places during the summer of 1863. Here he is (extreme right) with representatives of most of the European governments at Trenton Falls.

The South, with its constitutional provision for low tariff and the opportunities its cotton offered to foreign shipping, had strong friends in England and France, and it was only by cautious maneuvering during the first two years that Seward prevented recognition of the Confederacy. Not until the Emancipation Proclamation did pro-Union sentiment become surely established in England. After that the British professed to loathe the very idea of Victoria's "pure, matronly, and widowed hand" being kissed by the representatives "of so foul a conspiracy against civilization, humanity, and God" as slavery (Newman Hall's speech at the Great Union and Emancipation meeting, London, January 29, 1863).

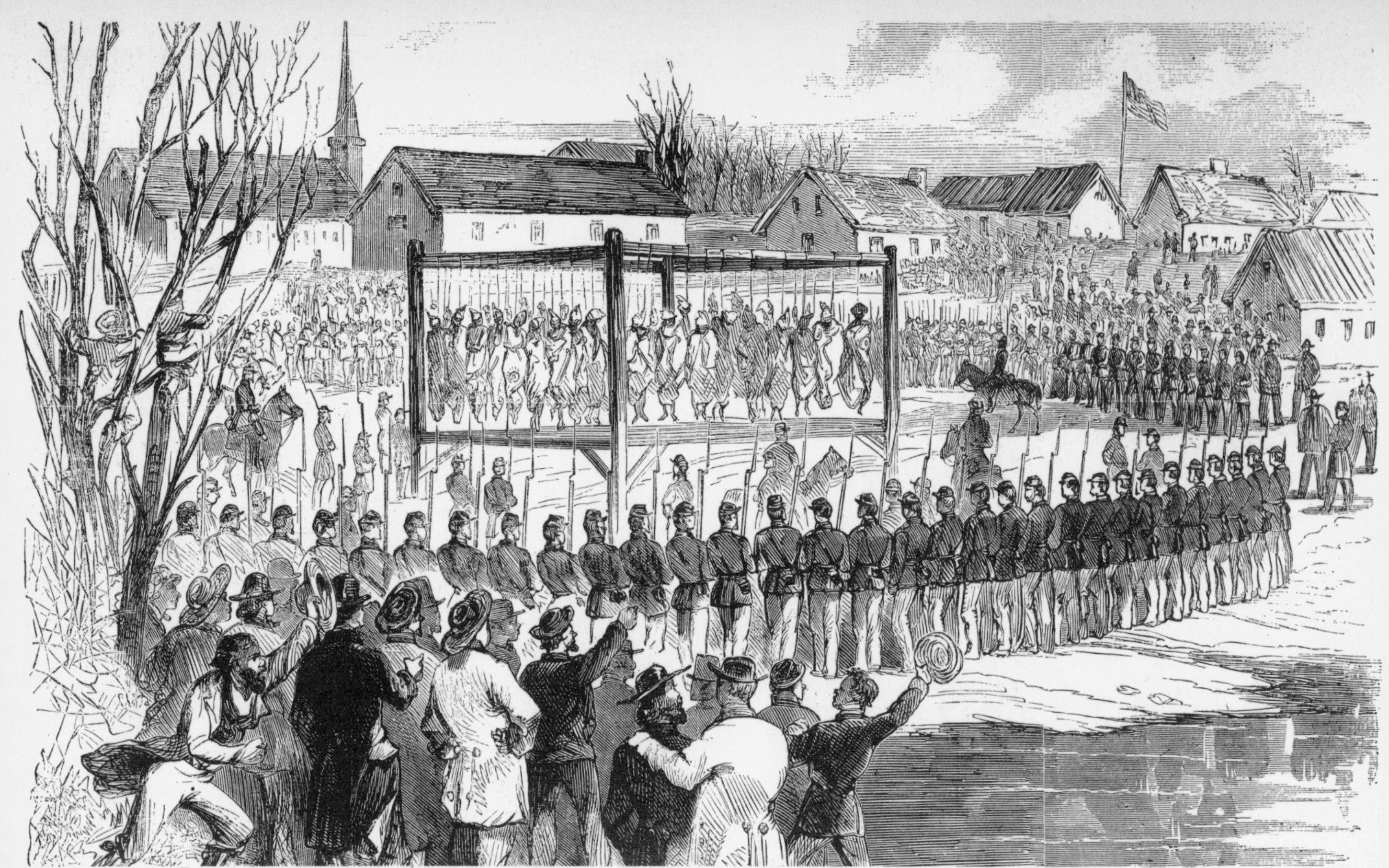

Mr. Herman of St. Paul

85. Along another diplomatic front there were also difficulties. Treaties with the plains Indians were constantly violated, and prospectors and settlers were crowding into the red man's territory. The Sioux of southwestern Minnesota had vacated much of their hunting-ground in return for a government promise of annuity payments, but so long were those payments delayed that the Indians, faced with starvation, raided the white settlements and precipitated barbarous warfare. Here are thirty-eight Indians who did not starve. They were captured and hanged from a single gallows.

Barnum's American Museum.
MISS LAVINIA WARREN,

THE LITTLE QUEEN OF BEAUTY,
will positively be
Married to General Tom Thumb,
TUESDAY, FEBRUARY 10,
and certainly closes her public exhibition on Saturday, February 7th.
This is the last chance of seeing her. She is on exhibition every day, from 10 A.M. till 10 P.M., till then. Admission **25** cents ; Children under 10, **15** cents.

86. Amid all the violence of those years P. T. Barnum still found an eager market for his marvels, and when his prize midget, General Tom Thumb, succumbed to Miss Lavinia Warren's thirty-two inches of feminine charm, Barnum advertised the romance throughout the land.

Thomas Nast

87. Winter found the usual crowds of skaters on Northern ponds, and the proprietors of near-by refreshment pavilions did a thriving business. Hot coffee and a warm stove were more important than secession and slavery to young people with cold toes and stinging cheeks.

88. Hot coffee would also have been welcome to the hundred people on this Michigan Central train. Caught in a blizzard while en route for Chicago, it was unable to push through the ten-foot drifts of snow. The passengers huddled about the stoves, piling in so much wood that the cars caught fire. When help came twenty-four hours later there was only one car left and the supply of wood was almost exhausted.

THE FINEST FARMING LANDS
WHEAT
CORN
COTTON
FRUITS & VEGETABLES

EQUAL TO ANY IN THE WORLD!!!
MAY BE PROCURED
At FROM $8 to $12 PER ACRE.
Near Markets, Schools, Railroads, Churches, and all the blessings of Civilization.
1,200,000 Acres, in Farms of 40, 80, 120, 160 Acres and upwards, in ILLINOIS, the Garden State of America.

The Illinois Central Railroad Company offer, ON LONG CREDIT, *the beautiful and fertile* PRAIRIE LANDS *lying along the whole line of their Railroad,* 700 MILES IN LENGTH, *upon the most Favorable Terms, for enabling Farmers, Manufacturers, Mechanics, and Workingmen to make for themselves and their families a competency, and a* HOME *they can call* THEIR OWN, *as will appear from the following statements:*

89. Railroads were prosperous ventures in those days. Regarded as an almost unmixed blessing to the nation, they were aided by Federal loans, subsidies, and land grants. Altogether the government gave them almost as much land as there is in Texas, and state governments were only slightly less generous. The Illinois Central got two and a half million acres, and by 1857 half had been sold to settlers at a profit of fourteen million dollars. Throughout the war years railroads were issuing advertisements like this.

90. There was also money for the railroads in the industrial boom which accompanied the war. In addition to carrying unprecedented quantities of coal, iron, and manufactured goods, they were carrying hordes of travelers to the cities. Chicago and New York swarmed with visitors, many of them merchants in quest of goods to replenish their stock. Out in St. Louis, where whisky distillers had already laid the profitable foundations of their fabulous "ring," there were visitors enough to require a hotel costing a million and a half dollars. Three thousand persons attended the opening celebration at the Lindell and marveled at its twenty-seven acres of plastering, its thirty-two miles of bell wire.

91. Typical of the rapid expansion of mercantile enterprise was the development of the ready-made clothing trade. Limited before the war to a few small concerns, it quickly became a huge industry with enormous government contracts for soldiers' uniforms. By 1864 almost 100,000 operatives were employed by the one hundred firms in New York City alone, and advertisements of gentlemen's ready-made fashions appeared in the best journals.

Under the stimulus of such business prosperity and of paper money, prices mounted steadily.

92. Raw materials and natural resources were also busily exploited. Most startling was the career of petroleum, known before 1860 only as "Seneca Oil," a patent medicine and cure-all which was laboriously gathered from Pennsylvania streams. In an effort to increase the supply for medicinal purposes Colonel E. J. Drake sank a well at Titusville, Pennsylvania, in August, 1859, and in the next four months collected two thousand barrels.

Quickly discovering the value of petroleum as a source of light, promoters riddled Pennsylvania with wells. By 1865, when this picture of Titusville was made, the state was producing three and a half million barrels, worth a quarter as much as the nation's wheat crop.

93. This war-time prosperity meant halcyon days for the speculator. Stocks in general rose an average of forty per cent in 1862. Brokers set up shops by the hundreds. The stock of one coal company rose from ten dollars a share before the war to two hundred dollars in 1864 and in a single year paid dividends amounting to two-thirds of its capital.

The frenzy was so great that the New York Stock Exchange did not offer sufficient scope to speculators, and in 1862 a man named Gallagher opened a night exchange in the basement of the Fifth Avenue Hotel. So prosperous was this stock-gambling venture that in 1865 a separate building was erected to house it. Then, a few months later when the Ketchum scandal broke, the regular Stock Exchange voted unanimously to suspend any member who attended Gallagher's, and the *Weekly* rejoiced at the death of the pestilent institution which "led directly to so many defalcations, frauds, failures, forgeries, and other rascalities."

CHARGE OF THE POLICE ON THE RIOTERS AT THE "TRIBUNE" OFFICE.

SACKING A DRUG STORE IN SECOND AVENUE.

HANGING A NEGRO IN CLARKSON STREET.

94. Prodded by giddy prosperity and inflation of the currency, prices rose more than one hundred per cent during the war; but wages rose less than fifty per cent. This resulted in considerable suffering among laborers, who began to defend themselves with unions. Organizations of miners, locomotive engineers, cigar-makers, iron-molders, bricklayers, and masons came into national prominence.

The draft riots in New York in July, 1863, were a formidable symptom of industrial unrest. Congress had recently passed a Conscription Act to swell the army's ranks, and when the first drawing was made on July 11th a number of Irish-American longshoremen were drafted. All might have gone peacefully but for the fact that these longshoremen had struck for higher wages, and their places had been taken by negro strikebreakers. Naturally unwilling to fight for the freedom of a race whose members had taken their jobs, they were in dangerous mood. A mob attacked the conscription office, and violence spread. Soon a gin-soaked mob was burning buildings, hanging negroes from lamp-posts, shooting and beating people to death, and looting stores. Police and militia were powerless. Nearly a thousand people were killed, and the damage to property was counted in millions of dollars.

95. But business still flourished, in spite of such disorders. The government was handing out contracts for uniforms, guns, food, and ships. At W. H. Webb's famous New York shipyard men were at work on naval vessels, and naval contracts were as prosperous as others. A captured blockade-runner, for instance, was sold at auction by the government for $12,000 and then leased from the purchaser by the navy at $12,000 per month. To be sure, thousands of lives were being lost in this war, but thousands of dollars were dropping into patriotic pockets.

96. Congressional committees were uncovering corruption in high places, and there was much that was not discovered. As the Federal armies penetrated the cotton regions of the South, fine opportunities for a little graft were offered to officers and treasury agents. From the wharves at Memphis, after the evacuation of the town by the Confederates, there was a brisk shipment of cotton and sugar to Northern merchants, who were appropriately grateful to their military benefactors.

Alexander Simplot

97. Meanwhile the fighting continued. A costly victory at Gettysburg helped to restore Northern morale after the bloody defeats at Fredericksburg and Chancellorsville, and a few months later came the battle of Chattanooga.

Then, in early May, 1864, Sherman began his campaign in Georgia. At the beginning of the war Federal officers made every effort to respect and protect private property, but in the summer of 1862, when it became apparent that only a military conquest of the Confederacy could preserve the Union, other tactics were intro-

duced. Having taken and burned Atlanta, Sherman set about systematically perfecting the policy of punishing the South. In his official report of the march to the sea he wrote, "One hundred million dollars' of damage has been done to Georgia; twenty million inured to our benefit, the remainder simply waste and destruction." Then he moved north into South Carolina, his whole army "burning with an insatiable desire to wreak vengeance" upon the birthplace of secession. This was the kind of warfare that sowed victory but harvested bitterness.

A. W. Warren

98. Then early in April, after a nine months' siege, Lee evacuated Richmond; the town was left in flames. It was Lee's plan to get supplies at Lynchburg and then join forces with Johnston. Closely pursued by Grant and Meade, he got as far as Appomattox Court House, where Sheridan's cavalry stood across his path. With only twenty-five thousand men left, less than half of whom had guns or ammunition, there was no longer any hope, and Lee surrendered. A few days later Abraham Lincoln was dead at the hands of an assassin.

99. Three months later another leader died. Edmund Ruffin, whom we met at Fort Sumter four years before (No. 52), loaded a musket with buckshot, put the muzzle in his mouth, and blew the top of his head off. He left behind him a note in which he maintained his determination to die rather than submit to the government of the United States.

PART THREE

A New Nation

1866-1876

A. M'Callum

100. Few Southerners followed Ruffin's example. Some irreconcilables emigrated to other lands, but the majority of those who had supported the Confederacy were ready to follow Lee's admonition to remain in the country, promote harmony and good feeling, and qualify themselves to vote. The Northern radical Republicans, however, were not to be placated so easily. Thaddeus Stevens was rallying them to "humble the proud traitors" by disfranchising all but "loyal" whites, confiscating land, granting the negroes immediate political and social rights, and thereby securing "perpetual ascendancy to the party of the Union."

Emerson, who had typified the belief that the war would bring true freedom in every sphere of life, wrote in his Journal late in 1865 that "every interest is found as sectional and timorous as before. . . ." President Lincoln's conciliatory policy toward the defeated South had been publicly denounced as a "stupid outrage" by the same radicals who now maneuvered an extra-legal conviction of three men and a woman for complicity in his assassination. So four were hanged for a crime which the most powerful leaders in Congress would gladly have abetted.

101. For a while, before Congress interfered, President Johnson carried out Lincoln's scheme of reconstruction. He appointed civil governors in all the Southern states under whose leadership constitutional conventions were held to restore regular civil administrations.

Meanwhile the negroes were floundering in their new freedom. They had been cared for when they were slaves, but now thousands of them were abandoned to the cruelly misleading flattery of political demagogues and to their own ignorance and carelessness. Believing that they would be given free land, and confusing liberty with the absence of work, thousands huddled in little villages like Slabtown, among the ruins of Hampton, Virginia. Here they lived in squalor and filth, ignorant of the means to combat diseases which in some districts killed anywhere from a fourth to a third of their number in a few years.

102. Immediately after the war there was a nervous spasm of prosperity in most Southern towns which raised false hopes. The pressing need for the commonest articles caused a spurt of buying, the money for purchases coming chiefly from the sale of reserve cotton. Gold, copper, silver, and slate mines were rapidly opened in Virginia, and their products shipped to Richmond over the same James River canal which had figured so largely in the mobilization of the Confederate army four years earlier (see No. 57).

Business houses everywhere were rapidly rebuilt or enlarged, hotels were crowded, and warehouses were scenes of bustling activity.

J. R. Hamilton

J. R. Hamilton

103. The Shockoe Creek Valley, Richmond, presented a striking composite of the Southern situation. At the left of the picture is the mansion which had served as Jefferson Davis' White House, a symbol of the patrician families who had lost everything. Winding through the valley is the railroad to Washington. At the time of Appomattox it was a ruin. In three months eleven bridges were repaired, eleven miles of track relaid, and all the depots rebuilt. But the fertile lands of the valley, like most of the agricultural regions of the South, were scarcely producing, and it was upon agriculture that Southern prosperity depended. Seed, horses, mules, and cows were scarce; plows and harness were patched or improvised. Most serious of all was the labor problem. Few of the whites had money to pay employees. Former slaves were crowded in a freedmen's village beneath the trees on the hill at the right of this picture, living on Federal charity, while the farmers of the valley were in desperate need of field hands.

W. L. Sheppard

104. By 1867 scenes like this, of blacks and whites together harvesting grain on a Civil War battlefield, gave promise of a new South.

Progress toward a solution of the agricultural problem came through the development of the share system. At first the planters supplied negro tenants with tools and food while the crop was grown, and then took two-thirds of the proceeds. Later the negroes supplied their own food and the crop was divided equally. As a result of this transition system the negroes were ultimately enabled to rent or buy land and set up independent farms.

A. R. Waud

105. In the meantime the radical Republicans were doing their best to throttle the South politically and undo the work of reconstruction which had been accomplished. There had been a frightful race riot in New Orleans as a result of their efforts to enfranchise the negroes for party purposes. Radical leaders had incited the blacks by prophecies that the streets of the city would run with blood, and when the riot broke, the prophecies were fulfilled. Soon General Sheridan was marching Federal troops up St. Charles Street past the famous St. Charles Hotel (center), and military government cast its shadow over the Southern states.

Theodore R. Davis

106. The most hated and feared people in the South were the carpet-baggers who came from the North with all their worldly goods in small bags made of carpet remnants, to seek their fortunes amid the post-war chaos. Resorting to the scurviest trickery, playing for the confidence of the lowest white elements while inciting the former slaves, they cheated and schemed for power. In the illustration above, one of these fellows is drinking in a cheap hotel and offering toasts to "Jeff."

107. Under carpet-bag rule the negroes were herded to the polls to vote the radical Republican ticket. The Union League Clubs of Philadelphia and New York sent missionaries to the South to teach a party catechism and organize the negroes into Republican clubs. There never was such a debauch of political injustice. "We'll make Arkansas Republican or a waste howling wilderness." The richest counties of Mississippi were represented by forty negroes who could neither read nor write. The carpet-bag governor of Louisiana "saved" $100,000 a year for four years on a salary of $8,000. The radical Republicans of Florida sold United States senatorships for good prices and then kept the money coming by blackmailing the purchasers. South Carolina had an Ohio carpet-bagger as governor and a drunken and debauched legislature dominated by ignorant negroes. Thus the orgy of robbery and injustice went on with blessings from Congress and the support of Federal troops.

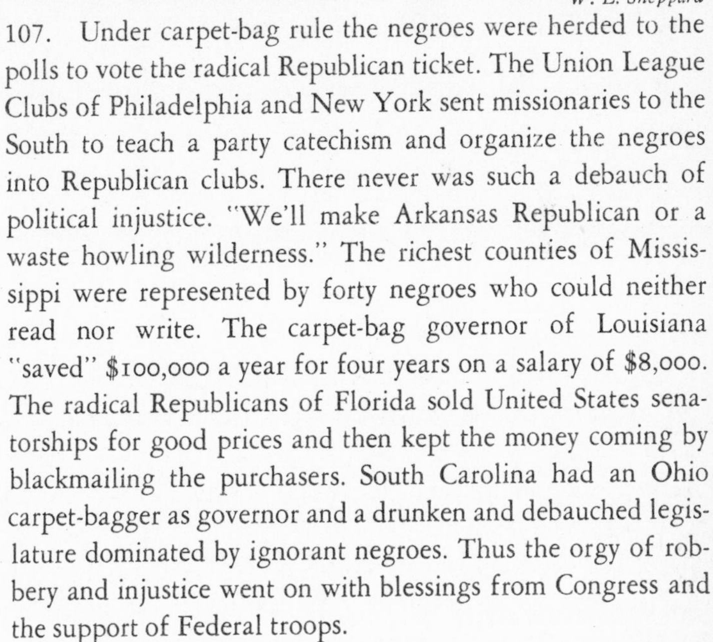

108. Driven to desperate measures by the ruthlessness of Northern domination, the white Southerners eagerly seized upon the possibilities inherent in the Ku Klux Klan. The Klan had had its beginnings in innocent masquerade, but it proved an effective means of controlling the negroes who had succumbed to malevolent carpet-baggers and for several years served a real need. Inevitably, however, the Klan became a cover for criminal violence, and long after its leaders disbanded it in 1869 its masks and hoods were employed in assaults and murders.

A. R. Waud

109. There is no way to estimate the social damage done by the radicals' methods of reconstruction. There are no units of measurement for the racial hatred, undermined morale, and festering corruption of those years. But some of the economic results are determinable. At the left of this picture is one of three mills for crushing the sap out of sugar cane on the twelve-thousand acre Millandon plantation near New Orleans. Each of the mills had cost about $250,000 to build before the war, and the owners had in those days refused a million and a quarter dollars for the property. After a few years of carpet-bag reconstruction they were glad to sell out for $300,000. And no wonder. While the state debt was multiplied by five in a carnival of waste, the impoverished citizens of Louisiana were ground down by taxes three times as heavy as those in wealthy New York. Similar tax burdens were imposed in other states, and the helpless people were driven to auctioning everything of value that they owned in an effort to survive.

Yet, tragic as the situation was, it brought about a fortunate revolution in Southern agricultural economy. Plantations were divided, in some states almost doubling the number of farms, and greater productivity resulted. The cotton crop of 1871 considerably exceeded that of the last year before the war.

Edwin Austin Abbey

110. In addition to the profits from agriculture the South was finding new resources. By 1870 there were one hundred and forty-seven turpentine distilleries like this in North Carolina alone, doing an annual business of over two million dollars. Textile factories, sugar refineries, tobacco warehouses, coal and iron mines, and lumber mills were growing sturdily, and gradually more and more people were able to dress comfortably, fix up their houses, and painstakingly obliterate the physical scars of the war.

111. When Grant had been mentioned as a presidential candidate in 1864, he had protested that his only political ambition was to be mayor of his home town so that he could build a decent sidewalk down the main street. The next year, full of honors and replete with glory, the victorious general returned to Galena, Illinois. Passing under an arch which bore the legend "General, the sidewalk is built," he was met by his fellow townsmen and presented with a completely furnished house.

Frederick Dielman

112. At the national capital in 1866 the politicians were only gradually realizing what a profitable and pliant tool Grant could be. For the present they were busy pitting Congress against President Johnson, who was anything but pliant. He had an annoying habit of vetoing bills which blithely ignored the Constitution and were designed to strangle opposition to the Republican party.

Here is the bustling scene at the Pennsylvania Avenue entrance to the Capitol after the daily adjournment of Congress. The horsecar went to Georgetown, and the train, bound for Alexandria and Richmond, may be the same one that appears in the picture of Shockoe Creek Valley (No. 103). Mingling in the crowd are men like Ben Butler, Oliver P. Morton, Zack Chandler, Roscoe Conkling, Ben Wade, and the emaciated but indomitable Stevens, who are calling the President a "tool of the rebels," a "mobocrat," and branding him as the leader of the Democratic party, the party of "traitors," "deserters," "murderers," and "thieves," the party which Morton described as "a common sewer and loathesome receptacle." In their frenzy for impeachment they would soon be bribing jailbirds to testify that Johnson had plotted the assassination of Lincoln.

Theodore R. Davis

113. Johnson fought courageously and never gave an inch, but even his attempt to appeal directly to the people was foiled by his opponents. They hired gangs of ruffians and thugs to howl him down and insult him from the audience. Then in 1868 came a day when the buildings of newspaper row in Washington were lighted late into the night. Telegraph wires to New York, Philadelphia, Chicago, Cincinnati were humming with the excited messages of Washington correspondents. The President was impeached—on trial for "high crimes and misdemeanors."

The trial was a brutal farce. There was no evidence to support the charges against Johnson, but the radicals saw no necessity for evidence. They could bribe or intimidate the judges. And it almost worked. They failed of conviction by only one vote.

Though Johnson thus remained in office, his influence over the government ceased. Congress was boss and went its own way.

114. Money was the only power to which most of our legislators would willingly submit. Their votes could be had in exchange for favors, and high tariffs and other legislative encouragements were showered upon industry.

It was not until the late 'seventies that the first full-fledged monopoly was hatched in the political incubator, but the time had already come to candle the eggs. When a successful Atlantic cable was finally laid by the *Great Eastern* in the summer of 1866, the company's office at Broadway and Liberty Street, New York, was promptly crowded with people willing to pay a dollar a letter for telegrams to Europe. There was talk of even higher rates. There was only one cable, and no newspaper or banker who refused its services could compete with a rival who would pay.

The *Weekly* was sanguine. "As for charges, the managers are practical men. . . . They know the immense value of their monopoly if the experiment succeeds. We must believe that they will not invite and actually compel competition. . . . If, however, they count upon competition as, in any case, inevitable, they will naturally make hay while the sun shines." That one word "naturally" gave a broad hint of the nation's future.

Winslow Homer

115. There were twice as many manufacturing establishments in 1869 as there were ten years before. This picture of closing-time at the Washington textile mills, Lawrence, Massachusetts, was typical of factories throughout the North. Prices were high, and there was a ready market for manufactured goods. Wages were higher, too. Yet the laborer soon found himself worse off than before the war. The cost of living had doubled while wages had risen only half as much. With two dollars' pay for ten hours of labor, the ordinary workman found his home growing shabbier and his food getting plainer.

Thomas Nast

116. Various labor organizations were formed to meet the situation, none of which was able to accomplish much in the post-war decade. When, for instance, the employees of a Massachusetts shoe-factory struck in 1870, the owner simply sent to San Francisco for Chinese who would work for less money. Chinese labor was a comet in the sky in those days. To the capitalist it was a boon, and it was not till twelve years later that organized labor was strong enough to put through the Chinese Exclusion Act.

Frenzeny and Tavernier

Robert Lewis

117. These Pennsylvania coal miners were members of a secret body known as Molly Maguires. Holding their meetings in deserted mine shafts or cave-ins, they planned campaigns of assassination and destruction of property as their contribution to the struggle for higher wages and better working conditions.

In general, however, there was little violence in the early stages of the labor struggle.

119. Many Eastern industries were succumbing to Western competition. Attracted by Chicago's Union Stock Yard, Armour and Nelson Morris began meat-packing there in the 'sixties, and together with Jacob Plankinton of Milwaukee they dominated the industry by 1870. In another five years Swift, too, was in Chicago, and the small Eastern packers had their backs to the wall.

118. Women workers suffered most because they were protected neither by unions nor by laws. In Eastern and Western cities they still worked for the same wages which they had received when the cost of living was only half as great (see No. 30).

To combat these degraded conditions the Working-women's Protective Association was formed, and Susan B. Anthony was put at its head. The picture shows a legal representative of the association helping a woman who has been swindled by one of the sewing-machine salesmen who made a profitable and dishonest business out of tricky contracts.

A. R. Waud

120. Westward expansion and the rapid development of industry brought about a vigorous extension of railroad facilities. Begun in 1864, the Central Pacific was pushed resolutely eastward from California by Stanford and Huntington to meet the westward advance of the Union Pacific, and in 1869 the first transcontinental road was complete. The building of this and other Western roads like the Northern Pacific, and the Atchison, Topeka, and Santa Fé, was a herculean task. The workmen of all nationalities sometimes lived on construction trains like this, which moved along as the rails were laid. Supplies had to be carried by wagons like those in the foreground. Indian attacks were frequent, and not all construction gangs were protected by a detachment of soldiers with friendly Indian scouts. Usually the laborers themselves were armed and did their own fighting.

A. R. Waud

121. Even in its first year the new Union Pacific offered passengers the luxury of this Palace Hotel car, and railroads in all parts of the country were improving their equipment. The average American road had cost only a quarter as much per mile as English roads, and there was necessarily a lot of improving and repairing to be done. Solid iron rails had to replace wooden rails with iron caps, and the iron rails in turn were replaced by steel. Coal replaced wood as a fuel, and petroleum products were substituted for pork as a lubricant. Safety devices were developed, accidents were reduced, and travel was made more comfortable. One American, traveling from Cleveland to Cincinnati ten years before this picture was made, found the cars "brightly painted, gilded, comfortably seated, and furnished with retiring rooms . . . ," while in hot weather "by ingenious machinery a constant current of air was cooled and washed clean from dust by being made to pass through showers of water" (T. L. Nichols, *Forty Years of American Life, 1821-1861,* N. Y., 1937).

Stanley Fox

122. Commodore Vanderbilt's New York Central System was going so well by 1871 that it joined with the New Haven road to build this Grand Central Depot at 42nd Street and 4th (now Park) Avenue. It was a monument to Vanderbilt's genius for business organization and a symbol of the wealth which scoundrels like Jay Gould and Daniel Drew used to bribe the legislatures and build their rail empires.

123. With the growth of railroads, the increase of industrial activity, and the growing stream of immigrants, the city assumed a new importance in the nation's life. The commercial districts of all urban centers were expanding, forcing the residential sections farther and farther out. Chicago was pulling itself up by its boot straps, raising the city's level twelve feet above the surrounding prairie; and cities everywhere were filling in swamps to increase their territory. In the picture above we look from Boston's Public Garden westward down Commonwealth Avenue. All this Back Bay section was made land, and typified the American city's unwillingness to be circumscribed by geographical limitations.

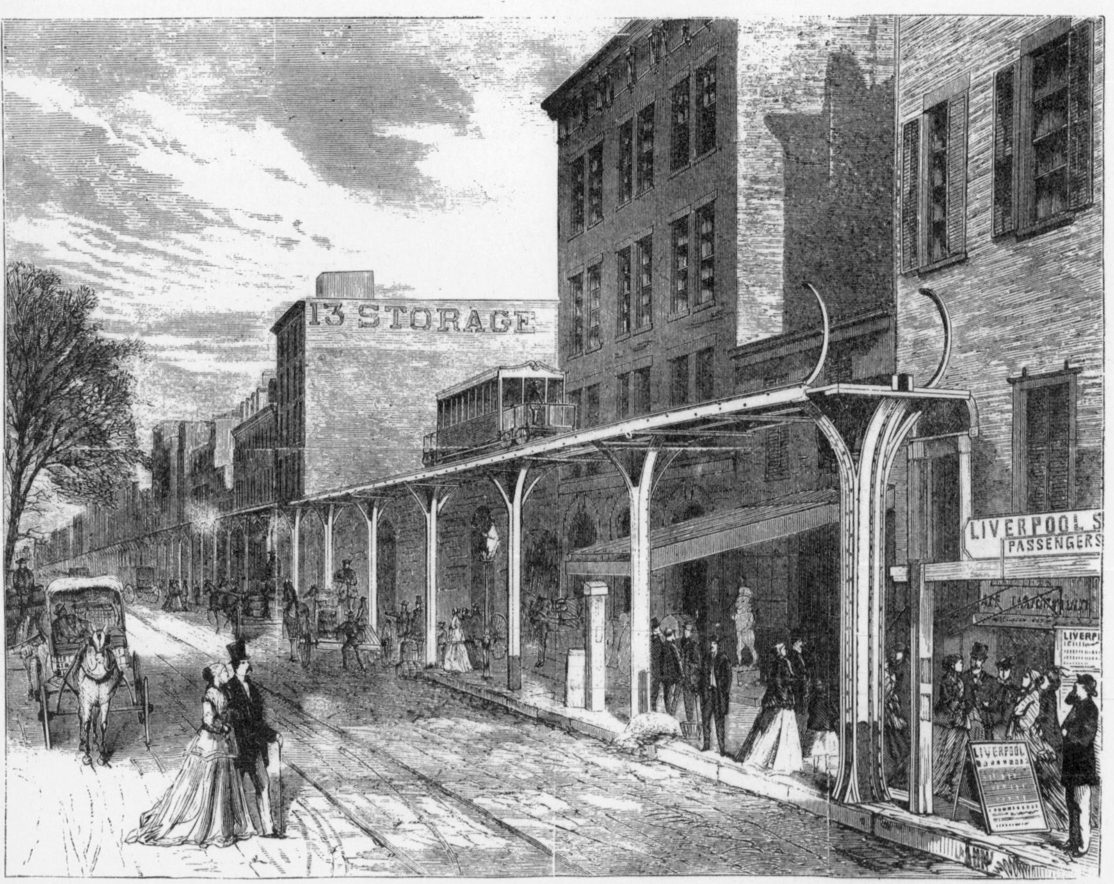

Stanley Fox

124. Rapid transit was a necessity in the expanding city, and on July 3, 1868,

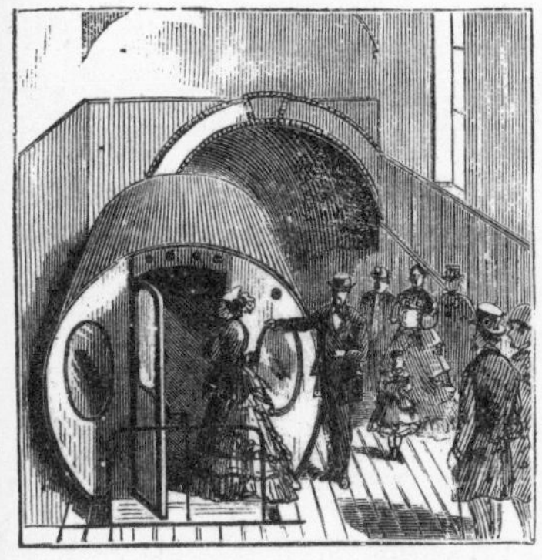

the first elevated railroad train sped along at fifteen m.p.h. from New York's Battery up Greenwich Street to Cortlandt. Within a few years two elevated lines were under construction on either side of the city.

125. As early as 1869 work was begun on a subway in New York, and by 1870 there was an under-

Stanley Fox

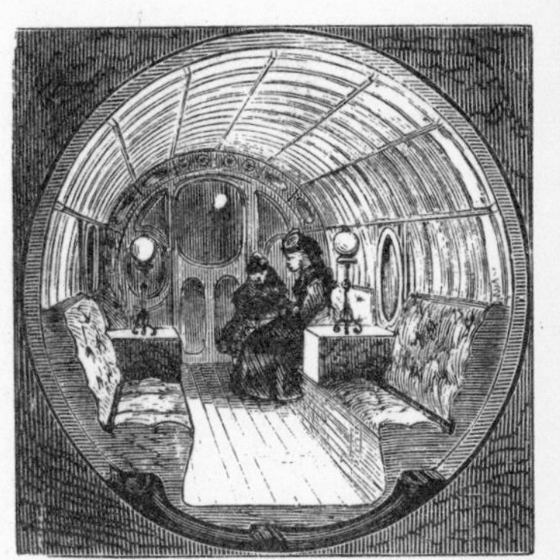

ground tube from Warren to Murray Street, through which a cylindrical car was alternately blown and sucked by a steam-powered blower. For two years adventurous citizens took demonstration rides for twenty-five cents, but the inventor failed to get a franchise and the idea of a subway was abandoned until the twentieth century.

126. Looking north from Pier 7 on West Street, the visitor to the nation's metropolis in 1869 had a glimpse of the coastwise shipping which contributed so much to the city's wealth. The side-wheeler *Stonington* (upper

A. R. Waud

left) was originally one of Daniel Drew's vessels. Jubilee Jim Fisk, Jr., made his bow to New York finance when he negotiated the purchase of this and other ships by a Boston firm. From then on he joined Drew and Jay Gould in the railroad fight with Vanderbilt.

127. This two-million-dollar marble palace was built in 1869 for A. T. Stewart, the great New York merchant, whose retail store had been patronized by Mrs. Lincoln and whose wholesale establishment was unrivaled in the land. Twelve years earlier Dr. Townsend's mansion had attracted gaping visitors to this same plot on Fifth Avenue (see No. 1). "New York is a series of experiments," commented the *Weekly*, "and everything which has lived its life and played its part is held to be dead, and is buried, and over it grows a new world." But Stewart's house, "if not swallowed up by an earthquake, will stand as long as the city remains." There is a great bank building on the corner now, and across the street is the Empire State building. Even Stewart's palace played its part and was buried, though there was no earthquake.

128. This tenement in Mulberry Street was home to eighty people, half of whom were children. Saturated with filth and vermin, strewn with garbage and waste, it was typical of the plague spots which bred typhus, smallpox, and diphtheria in American cities. In 1871 smallpox alone killed more than eight hundred New Yorkers and almost two thousand Philadelphians. As a result of these horrible conditions, health departments were created in numerous municipalities. Sewage disposal was improved, streets were at least partially cleaned, and tenement houses were supervised.

C. A. Vanderhoof

129. Even during the years when urban prosperity seemed to be at its peak, hundreds of citizens depended for their livelihood upon pickings from the refuse in the city dumps. These scavengers at the foot of Beach Street are collecting rags to sell at a fraction of a cent per pound.

Stanley Fox

Charles Stanley Reinhart

130. In the growing cities the pace of life accelerated. The leisurely restaurant did not satisfy men to whom time was money, and the quick-lunch counter took its place. Busy men of the early 'seventies hurried to "eating saloons" like this, had a quick plate of roast beef or oysters with coffee, lit their cigars from a gas lighter, and hurried out again.

W. Waud

131. This scene in Jersey City's Taylor Hotel illustrates one of the high points in the careers of Drew, Fisk, and Gould. Vanderbilt owned a large share of Erie Railroad stock, and when the three scoundrels began flooding the market with additional shares, he went on buying in order to keep the price up. As fast as the printing presses could turn them out, worthless shares appeared on the market, and Vanderbilt bought. When the three crooks discovered that the law was on their trail, they escaped to Jersey City, fortified themselves in the Taylor against the probable attack by Vanderbilt's hirelings. Barefaced bribery persuaded the New York State legislature to legalize the fraudulent stock issues, and the Erie was reorganized under the presidency of Jay Gould, with William M. Tweed and Peter Sweeny of the Tammany ring as directors.

132. The center of financial speculation was Wall Street, home of many of the nation's largest banks. The inflation of the currency following the war, the consequent inflation of credit, and the contemporaneous economic dislocations in Europe and South America combined to place the financial system in a perilous position. The nefarious schemes of men like Gould and his mates accentuated the peril. Immediately after the Erie reorganization, Gould and Fisk organized a corner on the gold market. With the aid of President Grant's brother-in-law they persuaded the President to hold back the Treasury's supply of gold while they bought all the available metal on the market. The price soared as the corner approached completion. Then on Black Friday, September 24, 1869, Grant permitted the Treasury to sell gold, and the market crashed. Half of Wall Street was ruined. Fisk lost everything. Gould alone had profited because he got word of the Treasury's plan in time to unload his holdings on Fisk and other unsuspecting friends, while pretending to buy more himself.

Winslow Homer

133. The inevitable result of such financial instability was the panic of 1873. Stocks suddenly depreciated a total of more than two hundred million dollars, and an era of aggravated suffering began. Many Americans are ready to believe that the lessons of the depression which began with the panic of 1929 are unforgettable. They might do well to read the article which accompanied this picture of lodgers in a police station in New York following the panic of 1873. They would find that during that year New York City alone saw nine hundred people starve to death; saw the Children's Aid Society providing shelter to more than eleven thousand homeless boys, while thousands more got no help; found three thousand infants abandoned on its doorsteps; found more than a hundred dead babies in ash-barrels, areaways, and dumps; watched thirteen hundred of its citizens die violent deaths; and had the disturbing knowledge that one out of every seven people in the city had at some time been convicted of a crime.

For several years the nation faced disastrous poverty. Businesses failed by thousands, hundreds of thousands of laborers lost their jobs, and disease, vice, and crime increased alarmingly. It did not seem that America could forget that lesson.

134. Though immigration dwindled after the panic of 1873, it never fell far below two hundred thousand a year during the decade after the war, and in 1872 it reached a peak of more than double that number. About two thirds of the total number of immigrants were bound for the Middle Western or Western states, but most of the rest swarmed into the great Eastern cities. New citizens were naturalized in the New York courts at the rate of one hundred per day during the fall of 1868.

Stanley Fox

135. Still figuring prominently among New York's foreign population were the Cuban insurrectionists. Their junta held excited meetings in these headquarters at the corner of Rector Street and Broadway. Here propaganda against Spanish rule was supplied for American consumption. Ammunition and arms were collected, money was raised, and plans for revolutions were laid. Several expeditions were sent out to the island in hopes that the United States would lend their support, but the nation was not yet ready for empire. That would come later.

Theodore R. Davis

136. The fire department in most cities after the war was a volunteer organization, hopelessly inadequate to the job of safeguarding block after block of buildings which invited flames. The complete destruction of the business sections of Chicago, Portland, and Boston in rapid succession brought about the more general adoption of fire-resisting construction and the organization of regular municipal fire departments.

Running to the Fire

137. The foreman of the Americus, or Big Six, Fire Engine Company in the days before New York abolished its volunteer department in 1866 was William Marcy Tweed. By 1870 this genial robber, with "Brains" Sweeny, "Slippery Dick" Connolly, and "Elegant Oakey" Hall, was in complete control of the city and state governments. Of the city's journals the *New York Times* under George Jones and the *Weekly* through Thomas Nast's cartoons led the attack on Boss Tweed and his Ring. Taking the tiger emblem of the Americus engine as a symbol of Tammany, Nast launched a series of cartoons which have never been equaled in power. It was not a battle of subtlety. "As long as I count the votes," boasted Tweed, "what are you going to do about it?"

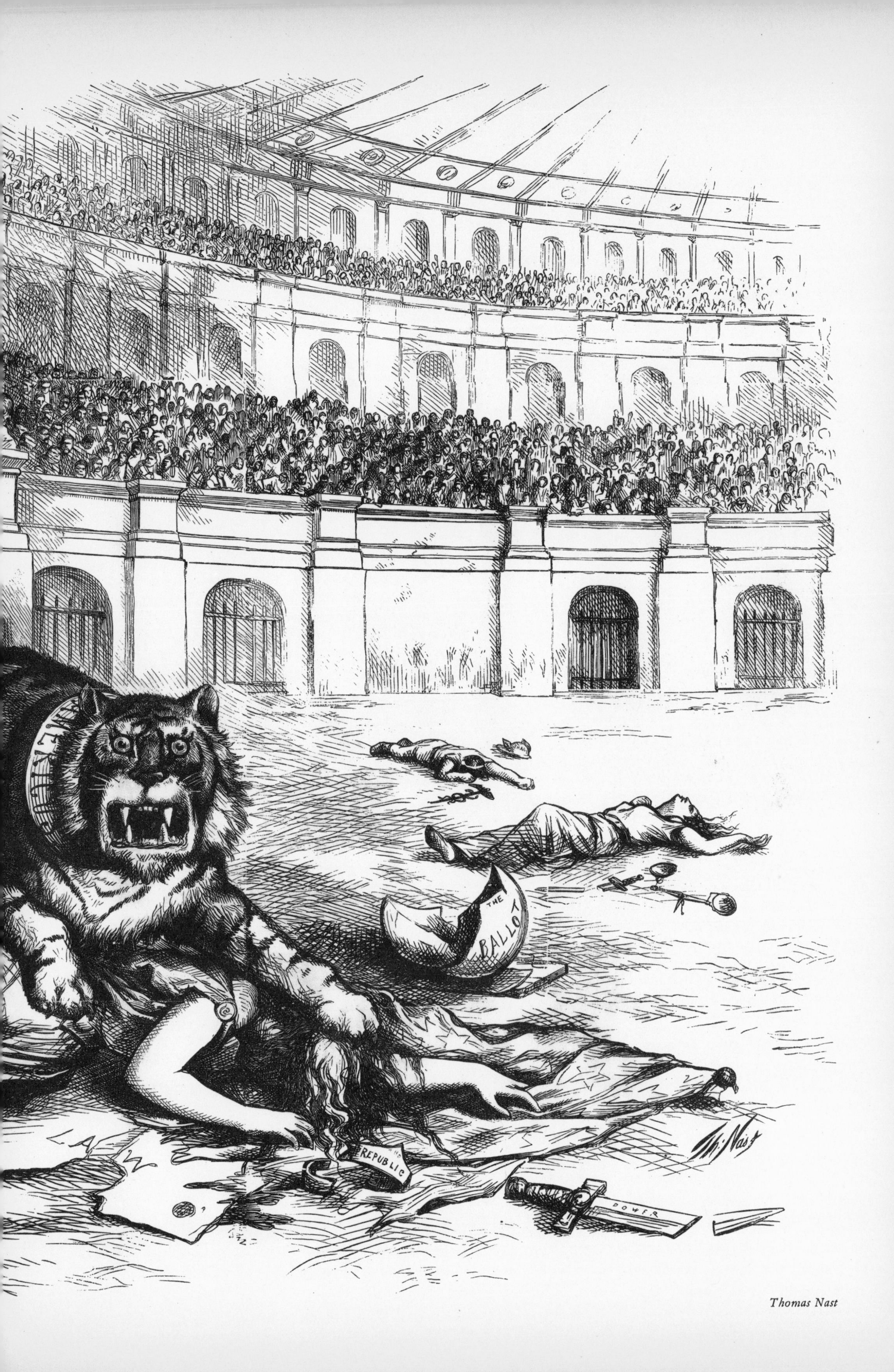

Thomas Nast

Thomas Nast

138. "I don't care so much what the papers write about me—my constituents can't read; but, damn it, they can see pictures!" So Tweed and his Ring sent threatening letters to Nast, and when they failed, offered him $500,000 to stop his pictures. Nast answered with more of his devastating and impassioned drawings, like this one of "A Group of Vultures Waiting for the storm to 'Blow over.' " (Left to right: Sweeny, Tweed, Connolly, and Mayor Hall.)

Stanley Fox

139. Meanwhile the *Times* kept on attacking. Its columns were packed with figures demonstrating the Ring's manner of looting the public treasury. One of the juiciest melons for the Boss to squeeze was this county court house, planned in 1868 to cost two hundred and fifty thousand dollars. The building was far from completed in 1871, though it had already cost the city about ten million dollars. Almost three million dollars were paid for plastering, more than five and a half million for furniture. There was a bill of $7,500 for thermometers. Anywhere from fifty to eighty-five per cent of these sums went directly into the pockets of the Ring.

Thomas Nast

140. The election of November, 1871, showed what the people were going to do about it. Tammany lost its majority in both houses of the state legislature, and the only Tammany candidate for senator who was elected was Tweed, whom Nast thus pictured with bloated and splitting abdomen among the ruins of Tammany Hall.

It was a heartening triumph over political corruption, but the purge was needed in many other places. Philadelphia and Chicago were in the grip of only slightly less spectacular robbers. The Crédit Mobilier and Whisky Ring scandals were permeating the national government with an evil stench, and the shameless pillaging of the carpet-baggers was at its height in the South.

Charles Stanley Reinhart

141. In contrast with the sordid story of politics and big business there was the work of a humanitarian like Henry Bergh. In 1866 he began the American Society for the Prevention of Cruelty to Animals, and the organization's influence soon spread over the land. This picture shows Bergh (in high hat) in front of S.P.C.A. headquarters with a wagoner who has been arrested for overtaxing his horse. It is an amazing fact that the prevention of cruelty to children grew out of Bergh's Society. In 1874 a starving, unclothed girl of nine, beaten and gashed by her foster mother, was brought into court as an animal, because the law gave no protection to a child.

142. The United States Life-Saving Service was organized in 1871, but for several years independent wreckers continued to patrol most of the danger points on our coast. The wreckers at Barnegat Light are here shown at work. The man at the left is carrying a cable, one end of which has been fastened on shore. The other end will be rowed out to the wreck in the dory. By means of this cable the life car (left of dory) will be drawn back and forth, carrying several people in its water-tight compartment on each trip to shore.

Having saved as many people as possible, the wreckers went about salvaging the cargo. Their only pay was a percentage of the salvage.

Granville Perkins

Theodore R. Davis

143. The camp-meetings of the post-war years were a symptom of hysteria, and great crowds gathered in places like this grove near Sing-Sing village (now called Ossining) to pray and sing. Especially after the panic of 1873 the country was ready for the exhortations of revivalists like Moody and Sankey.

144. The cause of temperance was fast becoming a religious and political crusade, and women led the way. These matrons of Xenia, Ohio, have recently left a temperance meeting in the local Presbyterian church and are now visiting Klein's "Confectionery and Toy Store," where ale and whisky are the chief stock in trade. Having sung "Shall we gather at the river?" they commence tearful praying, to which the voluble Mrs. Klein provides an indignant obligato:

"O Lord, we come not in our own strength ——"

"Shust git out o' my shop efery one o' ye. Ye're a set o' hypocrites ——"

"—that they may be enabled to see the wrong of this unholy traffic ——"

"Oh, I know dis t'ing fery well; it's like the epy-sootic. It goes all round und den goes away agen!"

Similar prayer squads picketed saloons in Dayton, Cincinnati, Zanesville, Chicago, and several Eastern cities. From such beginnings sprang the Women's Christian Temperance Union at Cleveland in 1874.

145. In a land where temperance, prison reform, and humane societies flourished there were naturally thousands of readers who loved Charles Dickens. More than a hundred and fifty people waited in line all night to get tickets for his reading in Steinway Hall during his 1867 visit to America.

Charles Stanley Reinhart

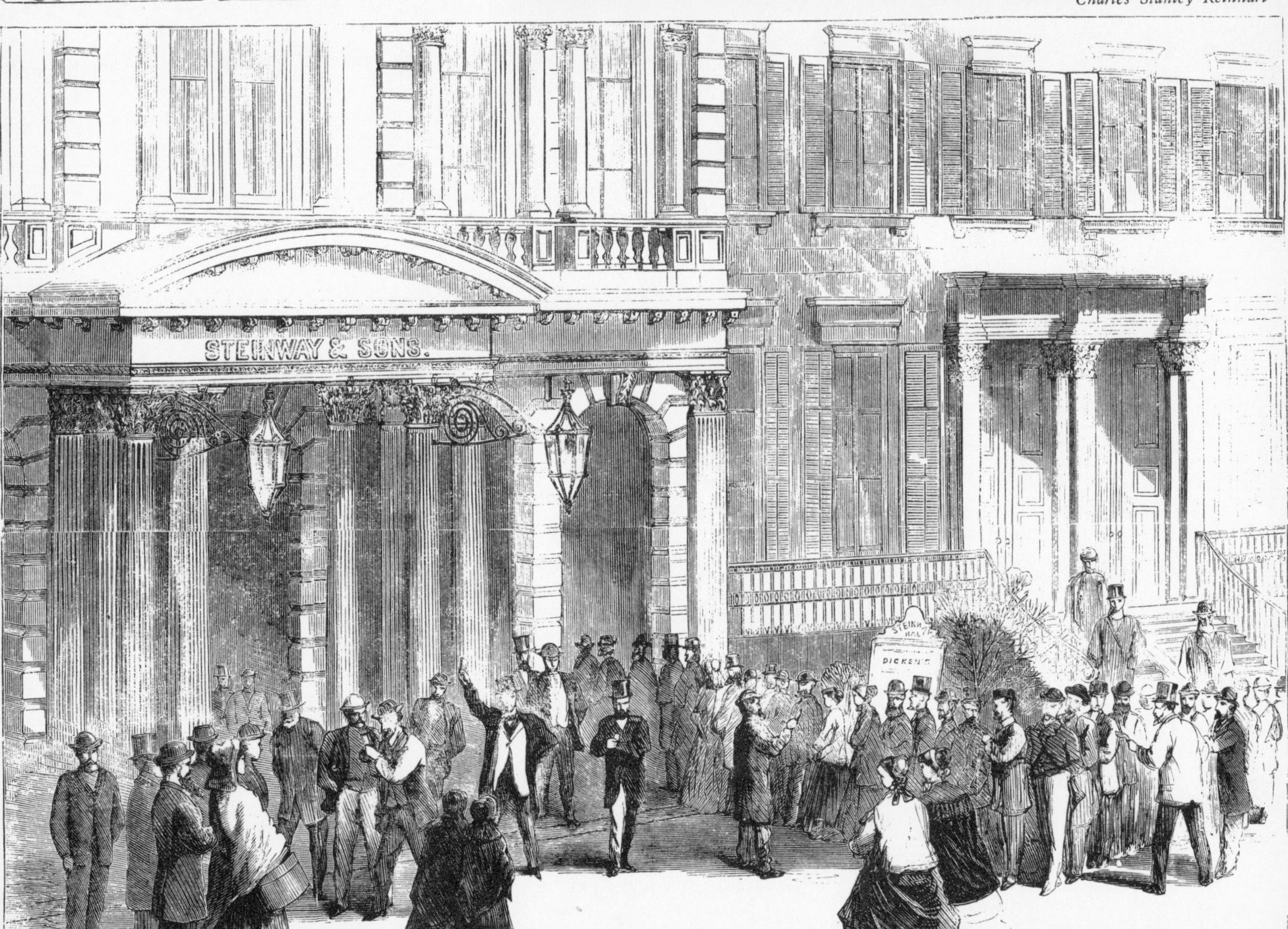

146. Much of the literary and artistic work of the period was little more than a genteel flurry of sentiment. The *Weekly* met the popular demand for "simple pathos" with pictures like this one entitled "I cannot sing the old songs now." Here, according to the accompanying lamentation, is "a fair girl, just passing into womanhood, in deepest mourning for one near and dear—it may be even for the life-mate of hope and love—checked by choking emotion in the first essay after bereavement to recall the melodies of happy hours gracefully spent. . . ."

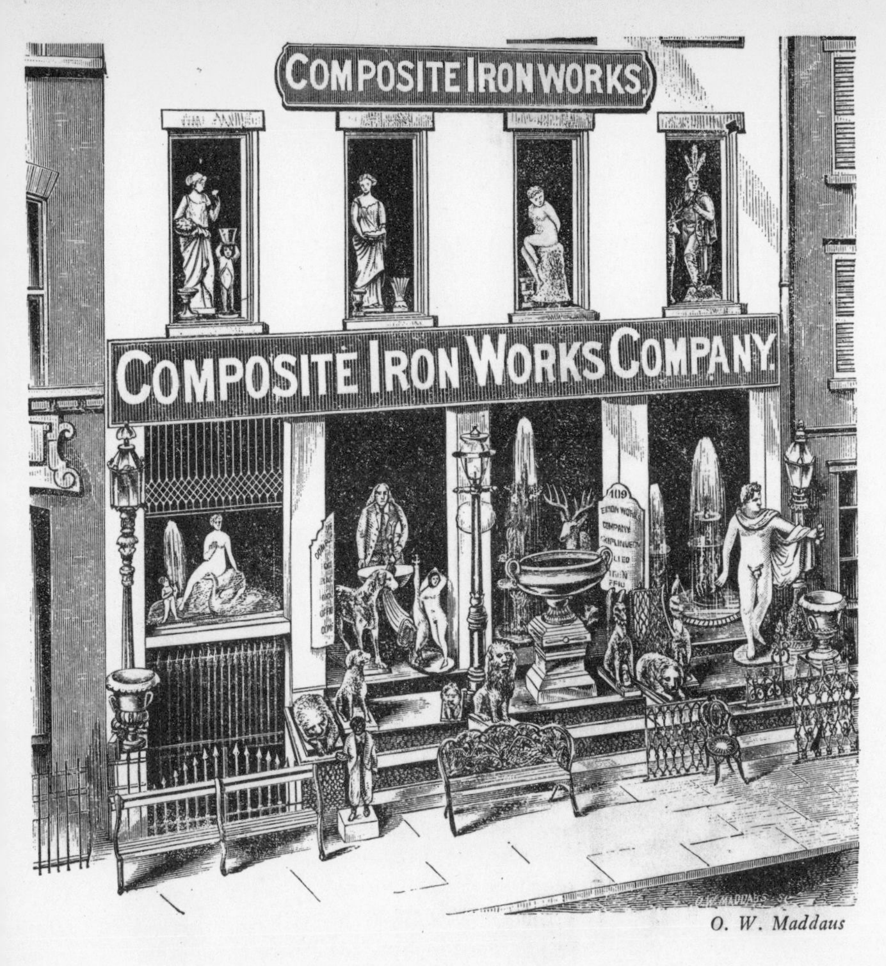

O. W. Maddaus

147. It was a decade of ugliness. Those who had money to spend spent it gaudily. Architecture became a nightmare of gloomy stone towers, mansard roofs, and jig-saw patterns in wood and iron. Furniture writhed and twisted in somber patterns of dark wood. The parlor was cluttered with lambrequins, antimacassars, plush albums, and what-nots, and the lawns of the well-to-do were peopled with ornamental iron vases, iron furniture, iron fountains, or iron statuary from shops like the Composite Iron Works on Mercer Street, New York.

148. This summer cottage at Long Branch, New Jersey, was built by President Grant during his first term and serves to illustrate what the *Weekly* considered "a very tasteful and elegant bit of summer architecture."

Ben Day, Jr.

149. Meanwhile new resorts were drawing increasing numbers to the shore for summer vacations. By 1867 there were hundreds of New Yorkers who took the boat to this excellent beach at Coney Island, where picnics and good bathing provided peaceful relaxation.

150. The annual horse-races at Saratoga helped to maintain the prestige of that resort. In fact, the horse-race was coming into unprecedented favor throughout the land. August Belmont, Leonard Jerome, and W. R. Travers were leaders of the American Jockey Club which built Jerome Park, and the presence of General Grant, Madame Ristori, and other notables at the opening in 1866 contributed to the fashionable acceptance of racing. It is interesting to notice, however, that Homer's 1865 picture of Saratoga is more concerned with the ladies' hats than with the horses.

151. The croquet epidemic began in the summer of 1866. Lawns from the Atlantic to the Mississippi were swiftly infected with wickets, mallets, and wooden balls, and expensive equipment from England was widely purchased.

Winslow Homer

C. G. Bush

152. Yachting increased in favor. This picture of the annual review of the New York Yacht Club was made from the deck of Alfred Van Santvoord's steam-yacht, *River Queen,* upon which President Lincoln had conferred, a little more than a year before, with Confederate envoys whose terms of peace he rejected.

Theodore R. Davis

154. The establishment of Vassar College in 1865, and of Smith and Wellesley a decade later, gave impetus to the higher education of women. Coeducation had been successfully tried in several Western colleges, and the old notions of female incapacity for advanced learning were gradually outmoded. Education in general underwent a democratic renovation: Harvard's President Eliot fought for the elective system; the land-grant colleges of the West placed a healthy accent on courses in agriculture and engineering and undermined the old system of sectarian control; and following the leadership of President White of Cornell and of E. S. Youmans, many colleges broadened their scientific curriculum.

153. College sports began to assume something of their modern importance. Princeton and Rutgers played the first intercollegiate football game in 1869, baseball teams practiced on every campus, and intercollegiate regattas were held annually. Columbia's crew came in first over the three-mile course at Saratoga in 1874, with Wesleyan second and Harvard (which had knocked the rudder and an oar from Yale's boat) third.

Winslow Homer

155. Yet education was still chiefly confined to elementary schools, and in rural districts of the North and West such schools were often poorly equipped. In the South the school system had almost completely collapsed. Only about three per cent of the seven million pupils in the nation's elementary schools ever got beyond the eighth-grade level.

Meanwhile the war and industry had drawn men from the teaching profession, and schoolmarms had taken the jobs.

Frederick Stuart Church

156. The multitude of small-town and rural newspapers which came into existence after the war also contributed to popular education. Many country editors gave subscriptions to their papers in exchange for turkeys, pumpkins, hams, and other farm products.

These rural papers were usually four-page affairs. Early in the 'seventies the Associated Press and other news organizations began supplying country offices with "patent insides" consisting of two pages of general news. The other two pages were made up with local gossip and advertisements.

Edwin Austin Abbey

157. Art had formerly penetrated the rural regions chiefly in the guise of traveling oil-portrait painters and silhouette-cutters, but during the post-war decade traveling photographers took their studios-on-wheels to the remotest towns and villages.

A striking indication of the revolution which photography wrought in people's pictorial tastes may be found in the wood engravings which began to appear in the 'seventies. Contrast, for example, picture No. 222 with No. 92.

Frenzeny and Tavernier

158. The traveling circus brought gaiety and amusement to towns and villages which had no theaters. Sharing with the county fair the affections of children and grown-ups, it definitely became a national institution. Far in advance of all rivals was P. T. Barnum's "Great Moral Show." Early in the 'seventies he introduced a second ring to his big tent and also inaugurated the practice of traveling by railroad instead of in wagons. (See the advertisement reproduced on the end-papers of this volume.)

C. G. Bush

159. Before the days of Sears Roebuck and Montgomery Ward the scattered homes of the agricultural regions were a relatively inaccessible market for manufactured goods. But when the war ended and the manufacturers were faced with over-production, they began to trespass on the territory of the old-time peddler.

Thomas Nast

160. In the late 'sixties the Grange, or Patrons of Husbandry, was organized, and by 1872 its more than a million members were actively engaged in coöperative buying in order to defend themselves against the grasping middlemen. In that year Montgomery Ward opened the first mail-order house, to meet the wants of the Grangers.

In addition to coöperation in buying and selling, the Grange assumed political and social eminence. Nast's cartoon refers to the militant uprising of the farmers against the railroads, which put a curb on exorbitant and discriminatory rates and laid the foundations for federal control as it was ultimately achieved through the Interstate Commerce Commission.

161. Stage-coaches still carried a great part of the freight and passenger traffic beyond the Mississippi. Butterfield's Overland in 1866 employed seven hundred and fifty men, a thousand horses, and five hundred mules to keep its hundred coaches moving. Ben Holladay and the Wells Fargo Company were even larger.

But the stage-coach was doomed. Indians raided the stations along the routes and sometimes attacked the coaches. (This picture by Theodore Davis was made from actual experience.) The coaches were uncomfortable, the trails rough, and the railroads were rapidly extending their tracks into the most inaccessible districts.

Theodore R. Davis

162. Except in California, Utah, and Oregon there was little agriculture in the Far West during the decade. Prospectors, like those here pictured in the Rockies, searched for gold and silver. When they found it, a

Frenzeny and Tavernier

hectic crowd swarmed to the new diggings, a crude and boisterous town rose overnight, fortunes were made and lost, and a stream of bullion flowed eastward or to California. Often the settlement disappeared as quickly as it had appeared. A new strike farther on ——

M. K. Armstrong

163. Agriculture throve on the great central plains. Here is the Main Street of Vermilion, Dakota Territory, in 1865. Since the passage of the Homestead Act in 1862, more than 100,000 acres of public land had been distributed to settlers through the little United States Land Office shown at the left. Between April and October of 1865 thirty-seven steamboats full of migrants came up the Missouri, besides hundreds of wagon-loads who came overland by one of the two government roads. They usually took comparatively small farms, worked them intensively, and made a thrifty living.

164. Stock-raising was also an important enterprise on the plains. Soon after the war Texas cattlemen saw the superiority of the newly opened Northern ranges for winter grazing; and when a cattle-market and shipping point was established at Abilene, Kansas, in 1867, great droves of cattle were driven up from the Southwest to be shipped eastward. Some droves, like the one pictured here, numbered as many as eight thousand head, and the journey required four or five months of difficult and often dangerous work on the part of the cowboys.

Frenzeny and Tavernier

165. Wichita, Kansas, which had been laid out by the land speculators in 1868, became the western terminus of the Atchison, Topeka, and Santa Fé Railroad in 1871 and immediately rivaled Abilene as a market for cattle. By 1875 it was the chief cattle-shipping center—a city with one railroad, flimsy wooden buildings, unkempt streets, an unsavory reputation of being "the wildest, and wickedest place in the West," and a few good newspapers. Of Col. M. M. Murdock's *Wichita Eagle* we shall hear more (No. 222).

Frenzeny and Tavernier

166. Those days of the open range, when almost all the territory between the Missouri and the Rockies was the Cattle Kingdom, were the last days of the Wild West. It was a spectacular life that the cattlemen lived. Law and order could be maintained only by vigilance committees who had no recourse to the courts. In this picture vigilantes are preparing to hang three horse thieves from a telegraph pole on the Texas border. One of the committee has been wounded during the chase; another is rigging a noose from the crossbar of the pole.

Frenzeny and Tavernier

Theodore R. Davis

167. Contemporaneous with the rise of the Cattle Kingdom was the destruction of the great herds of buffalo which had roamed the plains. As the railroads cut across their grazing-land the huge beasts became a target for sportsmen and hunters. Thousands of bales of hides and skins were shipped East, but many of the beasts were simply shot down and left to rot on the prairie. In the thirteen years after 1868 two and a half million dollars were paid for buffalo bones picked up in Kansas and shipped to various carbon works. The average price was eight dollars a ton, and it took about one hundred carcasses to make a ton of bones. That seems to indicate that more than thirty-one million buffalo perished in Kansas in thirteen years. It is not difficult, then, to understand that though a train could be held up for eight hours by a single herd in 1870, buffalo were almost extinct by 1885.

168. Women were scarce on the frontier. In 1865 there were four men to every woman in Washington territory, and Nevada and Colorado were even more predominantly masculine.

Distressed by this lack of genetic equilibrium in a district where a substantial population was needed, President Asa S. Mercer of Washington's territorial university took leave of absence in 1866 for a trip east. En route he collected about four hundred young ladies who were willing to emigrate as teachers, housekeepers, and husband-hunters. Here are President Mercer and a few of his companions on their chartered steamship bound westward on what the *Weekly* considered both a "praiseworthy" and a "suggestive" exodus.

169. (*See next page*) In 1876 the nation celebrated the one-hundredth anniversary of its independence by opening the Centennial Exhibition in Fairmount Park, Philadelphia. Even though many suspected, as did the poet Lowell, that America was unfortunate to be on exhibition when so much economic disorder and political depravity were in the foreground, the Centennial was a success. It was bigger than any world's fair that Europe had produced, costing more than five times as much as London's Great Exhibition of 1851. The Main Exhibition Building was the largest structure in the world, and Machinery Hall was almost as big. About sixty thousand exhibitors took space in the fifty available buildings. It was very exciting and quite surprising what a splendid showing America made, and about ten million visitors went home with new pride in their country.

See previous page.

Theodore R. Davis

Theodore R. Davis

170. President Grant and the Emperor of Brazil officially opened the Centennial by starting the great Corliss engine in Machinery Hall. It was symbolical of the new industrialism which had been transforming the nation since Lincoln's first inauguration. Machines of all kinds—looms, sewing machines, pneumatic drills, steam-engines, agricultural machines—were gathered in that building to impress the people with their gleaming power and polished speed.

Schell and Hogan

171. Some of the most striking machines on exhibition were the new rotary presses which were transforming the publishing business and contributing so much to the power of the newspapers. Here is a Webb press which printed and folded 15,000 sheets, newspaper size, per hour.

- Elm Ave. opposite Main Building -

172. There were probably not so many paid admissions to the educational exhibits at the Art Gallery, Agricultural Hall, and the various state and national buildings as there were to Shantyville, just outside the grounds. This was the Centennial's attempt at a Midway, a row of cheap wooden structures which housed variety shows, saloons, and such marvelous exhibits as "the learned pigs" and "the five-legged cow."

Yet there was much at the Centennial to broaden the horizons of the hundreds of thousands who traversed its thirty miles of exhibits. Walt Whitman saw the spirit of earth's activity and beauty "out from her evolutions hither come":

> . . . vigorously clearing a path for herself—striding through the confusion,
> By thud of machinery and shrill steam-whistle undismay'd,
> Bluff'd not a bit by drain-pipe, gasometers, artificial fertilizers,
> Smiling and pleased, with palpable intent to stay,
> She's here, install'd amid the kitchen ware.

PART FOUR

The Stormy Present

1877-1893

"The dogmas of the quiet past are inadequate to the stormy present."

—Abraham Lincoln

THE ELECTRIC RAILROAD.

173. Stimulated to new activity by the Civil War and subsequently bolstered by legislative sympathy, the industrial leaders of the country so altered the national economy that in the Centennial year the United States definitely took rank as an industrial world power whose exports exceeded its imports. Then came an era of invention and scientific investigation which further accelerated the trend.

The favorite electrical wizard was Thomas Edison, who was busy applying electric power to all sorts of machinery. One of his most interesting achievements was this electric locomotive which attracted many visitors to Menlo Park in the early 'eighties. The rails were electrified, the engine picking up the current through its wheels.

J. O. Davidson

174. In 1879 the public squares of Cleveland, Ohio, were illuminated by electric arc lamps, and during the 'eighties many American cities adopted the spluttering carbons to light their streets. Most of them used light towers at various points throughout the city like those which show in this picture of Savannah, Georgia. It was cheaper than placing a number of lamps on posts along individual streets.

The popular preoccupation with the inventions of Edison and other electricians was manifest in the advertisements of innumerable "Electric Hair Brushes," "Electric Flesh Brushes," and "Electric Corsets" in national magazines.

Charles Graham

175. Natural gas, in spite of early proofs of its cheapness and excellence, was very slowly adopted as a fuel and source of light. Findlay, Ohio, was one of the first communities to avail itself of the new discovery, and by 1885 its streets were thus flamboyantly lighted.

C. A. Keetels

176. The year after the Centennial Mr. Applebaugh of the New York Telephone Company was demonstrating Edison's phonograph at the Tribune Building.

Russell Thayer

177. Aeronautics still fascinated the inventive, and Mars was not slow to adopt Icarus as his protégé. This "dirigible balloon," invented in 1885 by Russell Thayer, was said to have a happy facility for dropping dynamite bombs, a facility which won for Mr. Thayer the commendation of the Army's Ordnance Board.

E. Meeker

178. Fortunately inventors were as busy trying to save life as to destroy it. Though Europe continued to carry patients to hospitals on stretchers, America rapidly adopted the ambulance after its introduction to New York in the middle 'seventies.

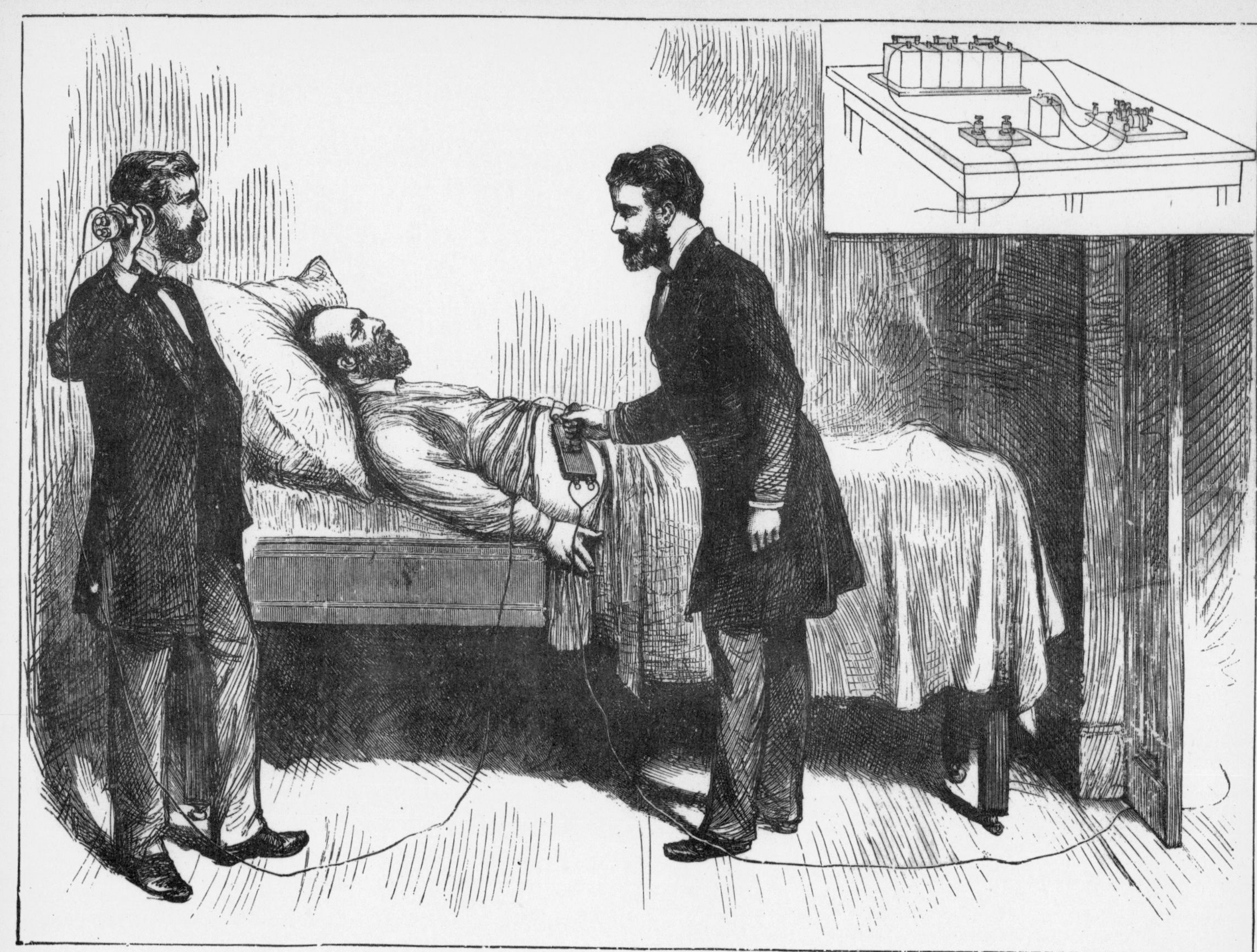

W. Shinkle

179. The telephone had been one of the most famous exhibits at the Centennial after the Brazilian Emperor casually put the instrument to his royal ear just as Alexander Graham Bell spoke into the transmitter. "My God!" shouted his majesty, "It talks."

In 1881, after President Garfield had lain for several weeks with an unlocated bullet in his torso, young Mr. Bell increased his renown by making an electrical detector which he and an assistant were permitted to apply to the suffering Executive. It was the first of the many contributions which electricity has made to the art of healing.

180. Not all inventions were dedicated to utilitarian or humanitarian use. Antoine Joseph Sax had made some ingenious contributions to musical art in the 'forties, and thirty-five years later his saxophones were being played by this popular quintette from Gilmore's Band before large audiences in Madison Square Garden.

J. O. Davidson

181. It was in the realms of commerce that inventions played the largest part. Typewriters, linotype, air brakes, refrigerator cars, adding-machines, combination harvesters and threshers, and countless other devices were either invented or brought to perfection during the period.

People were apt to wait a long while before they unreservedly accepted these new machines. It was almost a century after the invention of the steamboat before sails were abandoned as an auxiliary. First mastless steamship was the *Meteor*, 533 tons, built at Nyack, New York, in 1882.

Frederick Swartwout Cozzens

182. The industrial transformation caused by the application of new discoveries put an end to many previously flourishing enterprises. These whaling-ships, hove down for repairs in New Bedford, were part of the battered remnant of a fleet which had numbered more than four hundred ships thirty years before. By 1882 kerosene, natural gas, and electricity had replaced whale oil for lighting, and paraffin and stearine had replaced spermaceti for candles, and New Bedford's port was virtually dead. Those who had sailed its ships were now working beside their wives and children in the mills.

William Allen Rogers

183. Everything seemed to be changing. Hoboken's Elysian Fields were no longer a happy picnic-ground (No. 21). They had become a grave-yard for old canal boats, too slow to compete with the railroads. Squatters found shelter in the decaying hulls until wreckers came to break up the soggy timbers.

Thomas Nast

184. Yet Americans generally felt that the nation's hope lay in the expansion of industry. After Garfield's inauguration Nast drew this cartoon of Industry leading the reunited country in the ways of peace and prosperity.

Horace Bradley

185. Northerners enthusiastically hailed "The New South" as represented by Atlanta in 1887. Here, they said, is a Southern Chicago, built in a little more than twenty years upon the ruins which Sherman had left behind him. Eight railroads centered at Union Station. Hundreds of factories offered employment to its 60,000 inhabitants, and its cotton business was twelve times that of the last year before the Civil War.

Similar activity in other southern cities, celebrated from time to time by great Industrial Fairs, led many observers to feel, like Thomas Nast, that the States were being firmly reunited by industrialization.

Theodore R. Davis

186. This picture of a Bridgeport, Connecticut, munitions factory illustrates the change in manufacturing methods since the Civil War (see No. 59). In the effort to speed up production to meet the demands of European nations which were at war, hand work had been eliminated, and cartridges were shaped, loaded, tested, and counted by machine.

Charles Graham

187. The grimy, smoke-shrouded city had come to stay, and as early as 1878 Pittsburgh was among the grimiest. Here lived 90,000 people, and as many more sought the clearer air of the suburbs. One hundred and fifty factories turned out machinery and agricultural tools; eight plants turned out about 50,000 tons of steel a year. Three million dollars' worth of copper was manufactured yearly, and eleven million dollars' worth of glass. (The small insert represents Floral Hall, one of the buildings for Pittsburgh's Annual Industrial Fair.)

Charles Graham

188. These Bessemer converters, at work in Andrew Carnegie's Pittsburgh steel works in 1886, not only made better steel than had been possible before, but cut the price to almost one-tenth of what it had been. Most of this steel went into rails. In 1868 steel rails cost $168 a ton; in 1884 they cost $31. Because steel rails permitted heavier engines and cars, doubled the railroads' freight capacity, and lowered upkeep costs for roadbeds, freight rates dropped so low that it cost less to ship flour from the far West to New York than it did to deliver the finished bread from a New York bakery to local patrons.

Thomas Nast

189. Unfortunately, railroad rates were not always so low as they could have been. Worse still, they were not the same to everybody. Great monopolistic enterprises like the Rockefeller Standard Oil Company were made possible by deals with the railroads. The Erie and the New York Central agreed to give Rockefeller rebates on freight rates which were ruinous to competitors, while Rockefeller in turn agreed to give these roads all his business.

Subsequently the railroads themselves entered into monopolistic combinations and they became one of the most dreaded trusts in spite of temporary setbacks from the western farmers. So powerful were the Congressional railroad lobbies during their fight against the proposed Interstate Commerce Commission in 1886 that Nast thus ridiculed the "Senatorial Round-House."

190. In spite of the manifest improbity of most railroads' business ethics, the gleaming steel tracks and the steel-shod monsters which followed them had a strong romantic appeal. Joseph Pennell's drawing of the Pennsylvania Station in Philadelphia is an early example of the artist's interest in machine civilization.

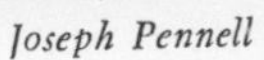

Joseph Pennell

191. One of the most spectacular features of the increase in the nation's exports after the Centennial year was made possible by the newly invented refrigerator car and the adaptation of refrigeration to shipping. Seven million dollars' worth of beef from the Western ranges was shipped to England from New York City in 1879, and very nearly twice that amount in 1880. Fielding would have had to visit Texas to find the source of the roast beef of old England.

I. P. Pranishnikoff

W. P. Snyder

192. Meanwhile New York, like other cities, took more and more of the surrounding country into its boundaries. Elevated railroads in 1878 were no longer one-legged contraptions like that on Greenwich Street a decade before (see No. 124). Two double-track lines extended far up the island. In the above picture we look east along Forty-second Street to the Sixth Avenue elevated station, the same structure which is now (1938) about to be demolished. Farther on, on the left side of Forty-second Street, is the old Grand Central Depot (surmounted by a weather-vane on one of its towers. See No. 122). Commuters from Westchester used trains to the depot and then continued their journey downtown by rapid transit. (The heavy, squat structure at the right of the picture is the Croton reservoir, which occupied the present site of the New York Public Library.)

Charles Graham

193. The process of consolidation and centralization which rearranged American business during the period placed Wall Street squarely at the apex of the commercial structure. The Stock Exchange throve, accordingly. A new building had been built in 1865, but by 1880 it had to be greatly enlarged. In 1865 there were four hundred members, and a seat cost $3,000; in 1881 there were three times as many members, and the price of seats had risen to $34,000.

(The electrically operated call board, whose flapping shutters have become one of the Exchange's most picturesque features, was first used in 1881, the year this picture was made. It is shown beneath the visitors' gallery.)

Schell and Hogan

194. Panic swept Wall Street early in May, 1884. The Marine National Bank closed its doors on the 7th, and people learned with astonishment that the failure had resulted from heavy overdrafts by the firm of Grant and Ward.

Grant was the first ex-President who had become a member of the Wall Street clan, and his name had lent dignity to the firm. Ulysses, Junior, was also a partner. But the active member was a young scoundrel named Ferdinand Ward, who used the Grant reputation to borrow huge sums for financing non-existent "government contracts." The president of the Marine Bank became an accomplice. Fraudulent account-books convinced the Grants that they were growing rich. On May 1st the General thought he was worth two and a half million. When the crash came the Grants found that they had personal assets of about $180, that the firm owed more than sixteen million. The General was old. Ahead there were poverty, disgrace, and disillusioned despair.

Julian Rix

195. A little more than a year later the General died. Meanwhile he had written his *Memoirs* during days of frightful pain, and Mark Twain was engaged in publishing them.

Strangely, yet in the American tradition, the long record of corruption during his two administrations, the almost puerile gullibility which had involved his name in financial scandal, scarcely tainted the nation's enthusiasm for the hero of Fort Donelson. His mortal remains were buried with brilliant pageantry in this temporary tomb on Riverside Drive just south of the famous Claremont House.

196. After President Garfield's death by assassination in 1881, Chester A. Arthur of Vermont became President and used his influence to extend civil-service reform. This drawing of the President is perhaps the first of the familiar pictures of presidential fishermen which now almost rival the navy in their popularity with rotogravure sections and newsreels.

197. Meanwhile the politicians had had a warning which they did not heed. The warning had come as early as 1877 when the employees of the four eastern trunk line railways struck as a protest against the second ten-per-cent wage cut since the depression of 1873. There had been crowds of jobless and hungry men on the streets for four years. The year before had witnessed the ruthless suppression of strikes involving Pennsylvania coal-miners and New England textile workers. Workers throughout the country watched in hopeless misery.

Then in July the conflict began. Without benefit of direction by the Brotherhood of Locomotive Engineers the strike spread spontaneously to almost all the lines in the country and even into Canada. Pittsburgh became the center of violence. The militia was powerless. Two thousand five hundred cars filled with valuable freight were burned at the Pennsylvania station, 125 locomotives were destroyed, both depots in the city were gutted by fire, and a looting mob controlled the city. Similar rioting occurred in other cities.

M. B. Leisser

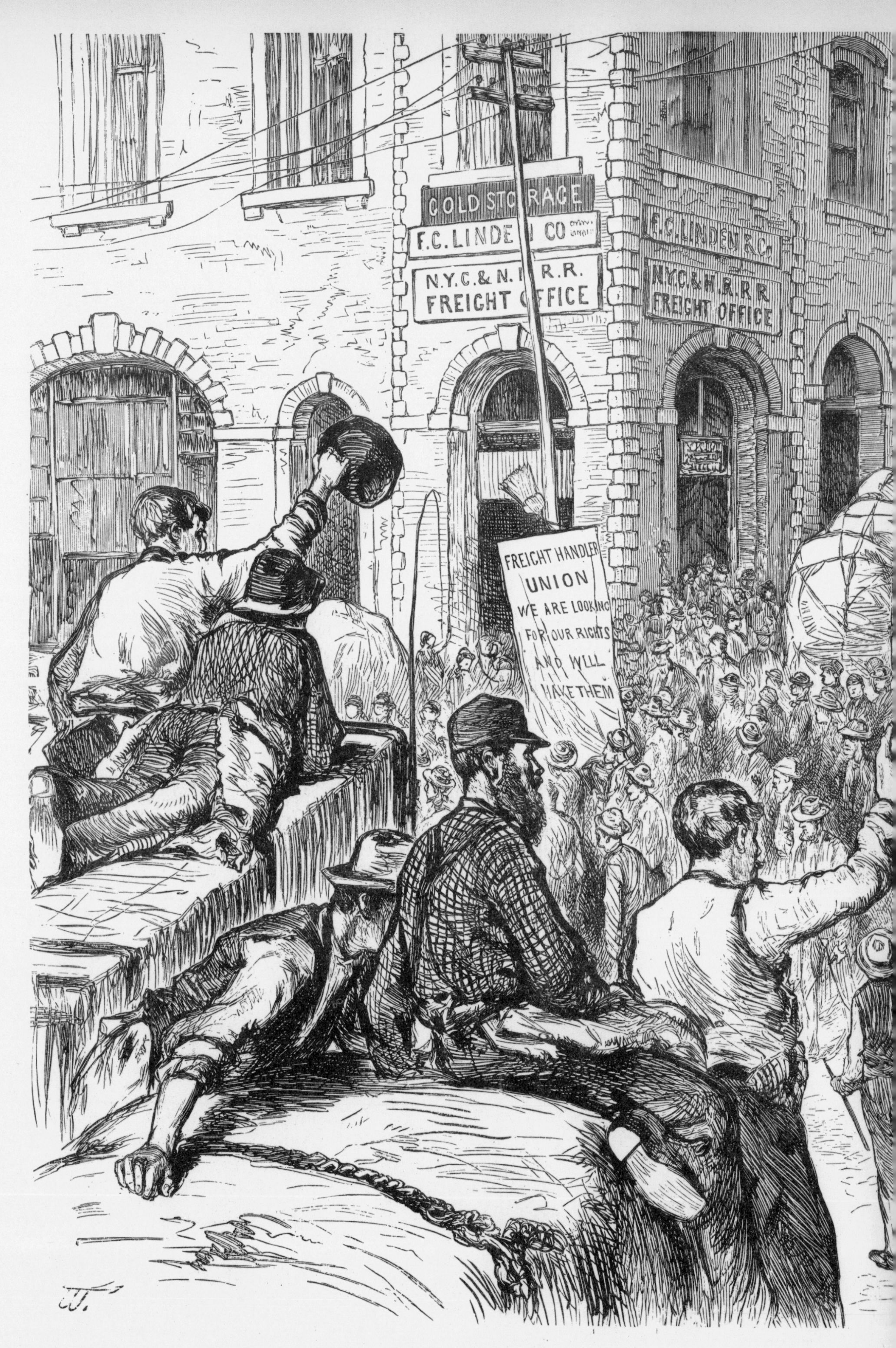

198. Though the great strike of 1877 failed to achieve its immediate aims, it did call public attention t the really desperate condition of labor, and provide the labor movement with a sense of solidarity.

There was general public sympathy with labor's aspirations in the late 'seventies and early 'eighties despit the power of anti-labor propaganda based on stories of destruction of property and mob violence. When th

C. D. Weldon

Freight Handlers' Union struck in 1882 and paraded before the freight office of the New York Central and Hudson River Railroad the *Weekly* reported an "orderly and creditable demonstration" in support of demands "so moderate and reasonable that it is surprising that they were not acceded to at once."

199. By 1886 the courts and the police had begun to take definite shape as defenders of private property and opponents of everything that could be construed as an "unlawful combination in restraint of trade." During the strikes in East St. Louis in that year it was deemed necessary, in defense of private property, for deputy sheriffs to fire into a crowd at a crossing on the Louisville and Nashville Railroad and kill five men

Thure de Thulstrup

and one woman, only one of whom happened to be a striker.

Also in that year, by a haphazard quirk of chronology, the Statue of Liberty was unveiled in New York Harbor, a cadet named John J. Pershing graduated thirtieth in his class from West Point, a man in France invented smokeless gunpowder, and Steve Brodie jumped off the Brooklyn Bridge.

200. A few weeks after the St. Louis affair two strikers were shot down during a May Day demonstration against the McCormick Harvester Company in Chicago. Next day a mass meeting was called to protest the shooting, and several Communist speakers were introduced. One of these, an associate editor of August Spies' *Arbeiter Zeitung* named Samuel Fielden, was speaking when the police arrived to break up the gathering. As they advanced on the crowd, a bomb landed among them, killing seven and injuring sixty people.

As the courts were unable to find the bomb-thrower, they decided that seven unquestionably innocent "anarchist" leaders should die anyway. Four of the seven were executed, one committed suicide, and the other two were later pardoned by Governor Altgeld. For this manifestly just behavior the Governor himself was denounced as an anarchist for the rest of his life.

This Haymarket riot heralded the downfall of the Knights of Labor's one-big-union type of organization, even though the Knights had no part in the riots, and it accelerated the rise of the non-political craft unions under the American Federation of Labor.

Thure de Thulstrup

201. By the time of the Homestead strike against the Carnegie Steel Company in 1892 the anti-labor forces had pretty generally succeeded in labeling anyone who disagreed with the employers' notions of justice as an anarchist. The *Weekly* sent a special correspondent and an artist to report on the group of anarchists in New York, and these pictures resulted. The picture at upper left shows Justus Schwab's beer saloon where, according to the correspondent, some of the milder Communists (terms were interchangeable) gathered to drink and sing. At right is the editorial office of John Most's *Der Freiheit.* Lower left is a sketch of Emma Goldman in what the police called "Tough Mike's Place" but which was really a barroom on Fifth Street just east of the Bowery known as "Zum Groben Michel." According to the correspondent, Miss Goldman professed to be the "anarchist wife" of Berkman who had attempted to kill Henry Clay Frick, manager of the Carnegie Mills.

V. Gribayedoff

William Allen Rogers

202. Anyone, whether anarchist, Democrat, or Republican, had food for thought in the living conditions which prevailed among the poor. This picture shows the accumulation of garbage, rubbish, and filth which was permitted to clutter the streets of New York's overcrowded Fourth Ward.

Charles Graham

203. Most notorious sink of New York's iniquity in the 'eighties was this tumble-down tenement on the north side of Thirty-ninth Street between Ninth and Tenth Avenues. Known as Hell's Kitchen, it has since given its name to the entire district.

In 1881 it was owned by Thomas and Catherine Wilson, both of whom were in Sing Sing at the time for engaging in highway robbery. The resident hero was Bully Morrison. Drunk or sober, he could lick anybody, and frequently did. Among the other tenants was John Mooney, who, when taken to jail (for beating his drunken wife for a night and a day till she died) found eight of his fellow tenants already behind the bars on assorted charges. Two hundred and eighty-seven criminal indictments were drawn against dwellers in Hell's Kitchen in two years.

204. Interesting as Hell's Kitchen undoubtedly was from both a social and an architectural point of view, visitors to the metropolis were more likely to be shown such mansions as this Fifth Avenue château which R. M. Hunt designed for William K. Vanderbilt. Hunt's flair for châteaux made him a very successful architect in the Gilded Age.

205. Another popular Frenchified building style was what the firm of Laver and Curlett, architects, defined as "a modification of the Louis Quatorze." A pretty example of this was the country home of James C. Flood, the California banker. A vast pile, covering almost three-quarters of an acre of land, it was possible only in a country where a man with a very great deal of money was happiest when a very great deal of it showed.

206. But, unsuppressed by the nation's taste for tawdry ostentation, there emerged more solid artistic achievement. Henry Hobson Richardson's sincerity did much to drive American architecture toward a courageous adaptation of materials to the fundamental purpose of design. Even in his early derivative work like this library in Quincy, Massachusetts, he showed some of his strength. He placed doors where they best served their purpose, and windows where they were needed, regardless of exterior symmetry. Yet his masses are balanced, and the building does not seem restless.

Louis Joutel

F. Hopkinson Smith

207. The Brooklyn Bridge, designed and built by the Roeblings, was not only one of the greatest engineering achievements of the time, but an artistic triumph as well. It made no attempt to disguise itself behind Gothic ornament. It simply spanned the river with the curving glory of its cables and steel, unequivocally a bridge. The picture is engraved from a water color made by F. Hopkinson Smith in 1881.

INNOCENCE ABROAD (IN SEARCH OF A COPYRIGHT).

"Then a sentimental passion of a vegetable fashion must excite your languid spleen—
An attachment à la Plato for a bashful young potato, or a not-too-French French bean!
Though the Philistines may jostle, you will rank as an apostle in the high æsthetic band,
If you walk down Piccadilly with a poppy or a lily in your mediæval hand.
And every one will say,
As you walk your flowery way,
'If he's content with a vegetable love, which would certainly not suit *me*,
Why, what a most particularly *pure young man this pure young man must be!*'"—PATIENCE.

Thomas Nast

208. Mark Twain, who perhaps more than any other author of the time saw the tawdry reality beneath gaudy surfaces, found it difficult to make his readers believe that he was anything but a humorist. So, when he went to Canada to copyright *The Prince and the Pauper* and found that authors must register their works with the Minister of Agriculture, people enjoyed the joke on the funny man.

Charles Graham

209. Although scarcely any significant writing was done for the American theater in those days, the stage attained noble stature through its producers and actors. Among the former was Lester Wallack, who in 1882 moved his company uptown to this new theater. The picture represents the theater during the screen scene from the *School for Scandal* on opening night, January 4th. The great John Gilbert played Sir Peter Teazle, and the beautiful, golden-voiced Rose Coghlan played his lady.

I. P. Pranishnikoff

210. American advances in science were certainly the most conspicuous evidences of cultural achievement. The government's geological surveys, led by the talented and dashing Clarence King, and the Hayden Survey of Colorado (one of whose pack-mule trains is shown here) produced admirable scientific reports based upon their arduous and adventurous explorations, and King's influence brought about the establishment in 1879 of a Geological Survey Bureau as part of the Department of the Interior.

Sol Eytinge

211. This sketch from Sol Eytinge's humorous "Blackville" series represents a negro debate on "Wedder Lord Dorwin involved hisself or somebody else" in his theory of evolution.

The spread of Darwinism in America was delayed by the Civil War and progressed thereafter less through the influence of *The Origin of Species* than through Herbert Spencer's and John Fiske's applications of the principles. The war between science and theology was raging by the 'eighties. Huxley's addresses during his American tour in 1876, and those of Spencer in 1882, were widely reported in newspapers. Evolution was discussed everywhere and became an integral, though sometimes unwelcome, part of the life of all intelligent people.

212. In spite of scientific upheavals and a growing tendency to dissociate religion and everyday life, the American churches continued to wield tremendous power. Out of the Methodist camp meetings which had been held during the early 'seventies on a barren New Jersey beach had grown the summer colonies of Ocean Grove (left of Wesley Lake) and Asbury Park (right). Good board and desirable rooms could be had for as low as six dollars a week, and thousands of people annually sought the tranquil pleasures of these resorts where no spirituous liquors were allowed and where the beaches provided not only excellent swimming, but also evangelical "surf meetings" which attracted devout crowds numbering as many as thirteen thousand souls.

213. Those who were content with more mundane pleasures during their vacations had several new resorts to choose from, in addition to the long-established colonies at Newport, Saratoga, and elsewhere. These men in sashes and women with collars and ties are on a hotel veranda at Alexandria Bay, among the Thousand Islands, during the summer of 1890.

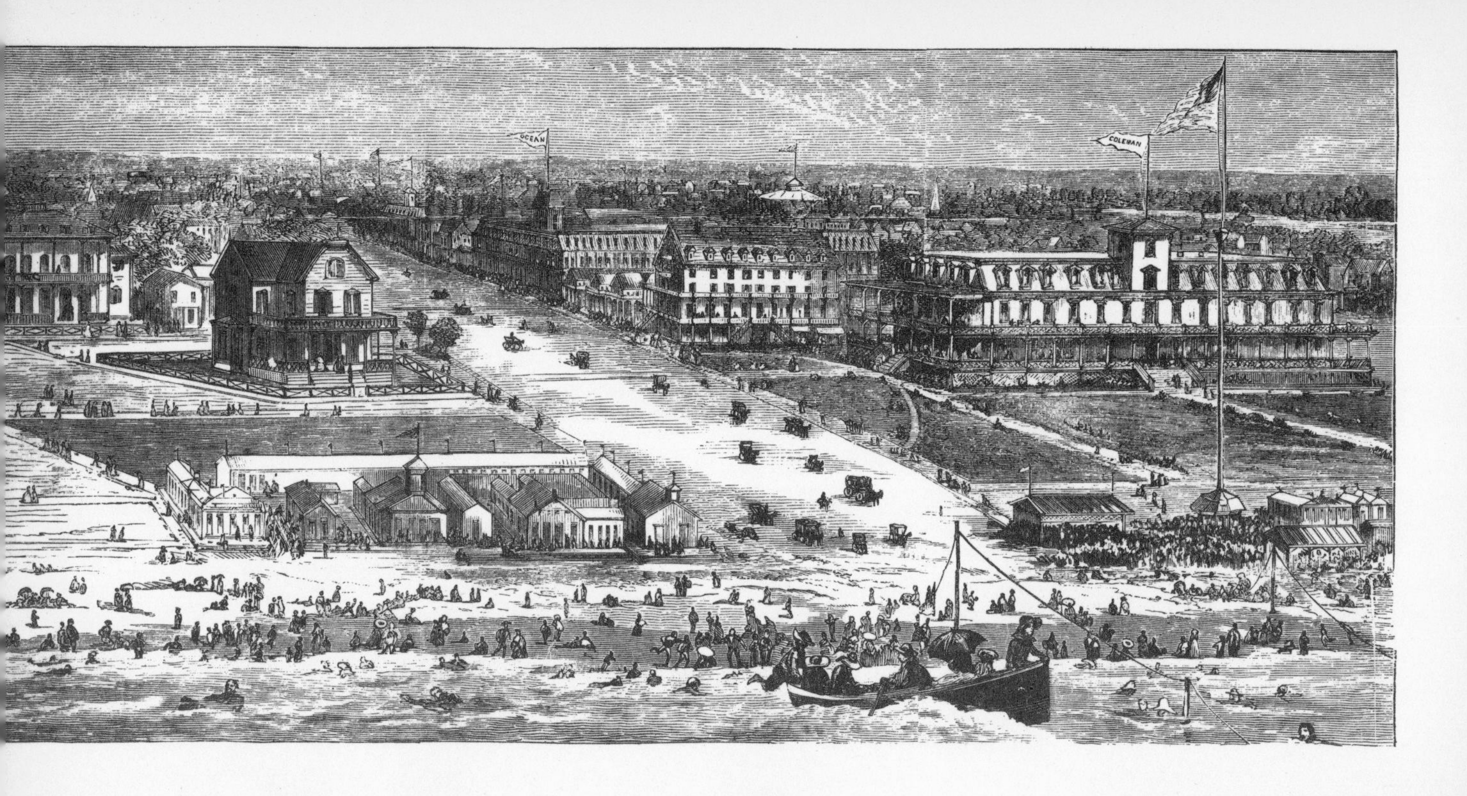

W. T. Smedley

William Allen' Rogers

214. Less fashionable, but more popular, than the Thousand Islands was the singular island called Coney. The peaceful beach of the late 'sixties (see No. 149) had in ten years become a gay confusion. Seven railroads and several boat lines brought thousands of visitors. Along the beach to the left of the observation tower the picture shows the array of bath-houses, pavilions, and eating-places. On the beach are shown donkeys which could be rented by the hour, a Punch and Judy booth, a strong man standing on one leg while he twirls his dumb-bells, and one of the resort's innumerable vendors (in this case a purveyor of dark glasses which were then, as now, in fashion). The vignette at the top shows the Brighton bathing pavilion which stood to the right of the tower and does not show in the large picture.

Frank Hamilton Taylor

215. As the passions of the Civil War subsided, wealthy Southerners began coming north again for the summer, and at the same time wealthy Northerners began going south for the winter. Handsome carriages and fashionably dressed promenaders appeared along the sea-wall drive at St. Augustine, Florida, during the winter seasons in the 'eighties. Dozens of Northern yachts wintered in Florida waters.

W. P. Snyder

216. Yachting, indeed, continued to increase in popularity, but it was too expensive to become a universal fad. More economical were bicycles. Late in the 'seventies bicycle clubs began to be formed in many cities, and the craze continued for two decades. Here we have the members of the Philadelphia and Germantown Clubs performing on Belmont Avenue, Philadelphia, in 1879.

217. Driving continued to be the favorite outdoor sport for sedentary citizens. So common did a horse and carriage become that the very wealthy turned to coaching in order to preserve distinctions. Colonel Delancey Kane originated the revival with a coach which he called the "Tally Ho," a name which has since become a generic term. Six members of the New York Coaching Club owned the "Tantivy," pictured here. It made regular trips to Tarrytown and back, carrying passengers for a consideration. The *Weekly* commended the coaching revival and pointed out that a coach and four could be bought and operated for a season for "a trifle over twenty thousand dollars."

H. Worrall

218. Fox-hunting also offered its romantic distinction to the wealthy. The South had ridden to hounds in pre-Revolutionary times, but for a century Americans had been too busy with other things and the hunts were abandoned. The year before the Centennial some residents of Hackensack, New Jersey, attempted a revival. At first their antics were greeted with ridicule, but other hunts were soon organized, especially on Long Island, and the ridicule vanished. Here we see the Rockaway Hunt gathered in front of Theodore Roosevelt's country home at Oyster Bay in 1886.

220. The great cattle kingdom of the open range was gradually broken up by a network of railroads and the barbed wire fences of the homesteads and sheep-ranges until by the middle 'eighties the industry had largely become a group of corporate enterprises, fenced and bounded, capitalized and directed in the East.

One of the most famous of the Colorado ranchers was a widow known as the Cattle Queen, who owned this ranch at Cimmaron. She had come to town in the early 'eighties with a little cash and her share of Western women's independence, and within half a dozen years, during which she managed the ranch and led her cowboys in the round-up, she had 15,000 head of cattle.

William Allen Rogers

219. Teddy Roosevelt had pursued other animals than foxes. He had been out West on a ranch where, like these Colorado cowboys, he had ridden a mustang after cattle and lassoed calves for branding.

Charles Graham

W. P. Snyder

221. The frontier was disappearing. In twenty years' time the government of Kansas had moved from the lonely shack at Lecompton (No. 8) to this elegant Capitol at Topeka. In the same period more than two thousand miles of railroads had criss-crossed the state; the seven hundred schools of 1867 had increased to five thousand; and the state's population had increased from about one hundred thousand to almost a million, a larger number than any New England state except Massachusetts.

It was in agricultural Kansas that the Farmers' Alliance became "a crusade, a pentecost of politics" during the 'eighties. It was Mary Ellen Lease, the "Kansas Pythoness," who toured the prairies at the turn of the decade calling on the farmers to "raise less corn and more hell." Here was the beginning of the last desperate struggle between agrarianism and capitalism.

222. Largely through the efforts of Colonel Marshall M. Murdock, editor of the *Wichita Eagle*, Wichita, Kansas, had grown in a dozen years from the crude cattle market of 1875 (No. 165) to a city of forty thousand people. Like many another Western community, it had been advertised as "the Bride of Fortune" and "the Banner City" by the newspapers and the traveling "boomers" who were paid by local chambers of commerce. As a result of natural advantages, aided and abetted by Murdock and others, Wichita had four railroads, sixty business concerns large enough to maintain from one to eight traveling salesmen, good schools, academies, and two universities.

Twenty years earlier there had been nothing but a land-speculator's dream.

Frederick Remington

223. South of Kansas, in territory which had been assigned by treaty to the Indians forever, lay the fertile plains of Oklahoma. But the white men had an eye for good land, and federal troops had their hands full trying to keep hopeful squatters outside the boundaries. In 1889 Congress and the President decided to give way to the inevitable. Why, after all, should we suddenly concern ourselves about breaking treaties with Indians? April 22nd was proclaimed as the day when the white men could help themselves. Blaring bugles gave the signal at the appointed time, and the stampede began. Guthrie, little more than a vacant site when the bugles blew, was a thriving city a hundred days later.

224. In 1893, four hundred years after the landing of Columbus in the Bahamas, America once more turned to a celebration of her achievements. On the Chicago lake-front the White City appeared as if by magic, with a notable group of architects and artists rubbing Aladdin's lamp. Definitely classic in inspiration and contributing very little to the development of a native American art, the World's Fair was nevertheless a thing of great beauty which rose surprisingly amid the stockyard commercialism of its time and place. Its greatest structure (shown beyond the lagoon) had the appropriately dual name of The Hall of Manufactures and Liberal Arts.

Charles Graham

225. Center of interest at the Fair was the Midway, with its Irish village, its Hindoo jugglers, its Ferris wheel (the first to be built), its village of South Sea Islanders, its Old Vienna, its Wild West show, its Algerian theater, its Colorado mining company exhibit, and its notorious Cairo Street. Here Sandow rippled his muscles at the fair visitors, and a young man name Ziegfeld was beginning his career as a showman, while Little Egypt danced in what Frederick Remington called "such a shockingly interesting way."

Thure de Thulstrup

It was no wonder that when Governor William McKinley of Ohio was asked for his opinion of the Fair he pointed out that it was "the world spread out before us . . . at a cost which is merely nominal" and that it consequently was (here an unintentional note of prophetic irony) "something which the people of the United States, above all others, should feel it an imperative duty to see."

PART FIVE

The Progress of Our Arms

1894-1900

Charles Mente

226. One night a few weeks after the World's Fair closed Charles Mente made this drawing in Chicago's City Hall. The stone corridors, filled with sleeping men who had neither jobs nor homes, were like a potter's field of unburied dead. A hundred thousand men in the city had no work. During the Fair the country had been hit by a severe industrial depression, and hordes of the jobless had collected in Chicago in hopes of getting work at the White City.

Only slightly less painful were conditions elsewhere. Prices and wages plunged downward, with wages keeping a headlong lead. Winter brought bitter suffering to hundreds of thousands, and rioting broke out spasmodically among citizens who were starved and cold.

Henry Hobart Nichols

227. This is not a picture of a peasant's hut in the shadow of some medieval castle, but a drawing of the corner of New York's Park Avenue and Ninety-fifth Street as it looked just after the World's Fair. The castle was the Eighth Regiment Armory and the hut was the home of an American family. Those were indeed hard times when even Mr. McKinley out in Ohio was tottering into bankruptcy. Of course the great Mark Hanna was on hand to prop Mr. McKinley up again, and there were even industrial giants whose wives provided soup-kitchens for families like the one beneath the Armory walls.

228. Within the walls of another armory, this one in New Haven, Connecticut, life still looked good-naturedly care-free. Young Mr. Walter Camp, who had chosen the first "All-American" football team four years previously, pronounced this Yale Junior Prom to have been "replete with jolly incident—a round of gayety with enough of the spice of lark about it to make it seem doubly attractive." He was also pleased with the typical prom girl, "a whole-souled, fun-loving young woman."

W. P. Snyder

Arthur Burdett Frost

229. The royal and ancient Dutch game of golf (for Holland seems to have been the birthplace of the sport) had for centuries found its most determined devotees in Scotland even though in 1457 the Scotch parliament had "decreted and ordained" that "gowf be utterly cryit down, and nocht usit" because it interfered with the more useful sport of archery.

It was fitting, therefore, that when the first golf club in the United States laid out a six-hole course at Yonkers, New York, in 1888 it took its name from St. Andrews in Scotland. Five years later the Chicago Golf Club completed the first eighteen-hole course in the country at Wheaton, Illinois. By 1895 a national golf association had been formed; courses had been laid out in several states; stymie, bunker, fairway, mashie, and caddie were becoming part of the nation's vocabulary.

E. V. Nadherny

230. Clarence Day's reminiscences of his father and mother have in recent years revitalized the life of well-to-do New Yorkers in the nineties. In this picture of the Stock Exchange in 1894 father Clarence Day appears in profile, second from the right in the second row.

F. T. Merrill

231. While women workers struggled to eat and pay rent and while farmers' wives raised blisters on their hands, most women of means held aloof in a parlor aristocracy where they were flattered and pampered. Circumcluded by Dr. Warner's corsets, they sat at tea and discussed suffrage, the purple passages of *Trilby*, the latest fashions, and their children. Many of them wanted to pattern their sons after the Frances Hodgson Burnett model and their daughters after the Gibson girl.

But these last years of the century were also stirred by such women as Julia Ward Howe, Lucy Stone, and Elizabeth Cady Stanton, who were seeking a new place for their sex in the nation's political and social life.

William Allen Rogers

232. Then in 1894 the smoldering anguish of the unemployed burst into a pyrotechnic display. The tens of thousands of men who were roving the country in search of work or food coalesced into several great armies. The largest of these, led by Jacob Coxey, set out from Ohio to march on Washington. The incandescent fierceness with which the ragged horde began their crusade paled gradually as more and more of the marchers dropped out. By the time the straggling remnant reached the capital there remained but a flicker which was snuffed out by simply arresting the leaders for walking on the grass.

The intrenched capitalists quickly seized on Coxey's army as a butt for ridicule. But the unrest which had been symbolized in its formation was not to be put off as a joke, and Rogers' cartoon in the *Weekly* turned scathing ridicule upon the "Original Coxey's Army" of industrialists who had been marching on the capital for years to demand and get high protective tariffs.

Frederick Remington

233. A few months later in Chicago six of the large World's Fair buildings and acres of railroad property were in flames and the United States infantry were in command of the city. The Pullman Company had reduced its wages by one-fourth, though it made no reduction in rents in its "model village" for employees. The result was grinding poverty for many of the workers, though the company had about twenty-five million dollars in surplus profits and had distributed in the past year two and a half million dollars in dividends on its thirty-six-million-dollar capital.

The American Railway Union, led by Eugene Debs, voted a sympathetic boycott and strike against all Pullman cars. The railroads' General Managers Association refused to arbitrate, and got a railway attorney named Walker appointed special counsel for the United States. Walker used the federal courts to acquire an injunction against the strikers, persuaded President Cleveland to send federal troops, ostensibly to preserve law and order, but actually to break the strike, and thus precipitated a violent conflict from which the employers emerged triumphant with new proofs that the courts and the government could be manipulated as they pleased.

234. Cleveland owed his election in 1892 partly to numbers of distressed farmers who saw in the Democrats more hope than could be expected from the new Populist party. Yet the Populists elected two Senators and eleven Representatives, and in the congressional elections of 1894 they made further gains. Populist picnics, like this one in South Dakota, and political "revivals" with speeches and music, whipped up enthusiasm for the free-silver panacea and stressed the necessity for a graduated income tax, shorter working-hours for labor, direct election of United States Senators, postal savings banks, and other equally "subversive" and "radical" proposals, almost all of which have since become law with the benediction of the conservatives.

Childe Hassam

Childe Hassam

235. In 1895, when the *Weekly* published this picture of the Prado at Havana by Childe Hassam, a new rebellion began in Cuba, and immediately the old thirst for empire was raised again in America. Spanish rule in Cuba was undeniably severe. In retaliation Gomez and his insurrectionists adopted the policy of crippling the island's economic life, chiefly by burning cane-fields and thus destroying the lucrative sugar industry from which the Spanish derived the bulk of the government tax revenues.

American politicians, faced with the energetic agitation of the Populists, and others who thought it expedient to divert attention from industrial and political unrest at home, began playing with the American people's historic sympathy for oppressed peoples. Yet there were some who knew, as did the editors of the *Weekly*, that "at the bottom of all the pretended sympathy for Cuba lies the desire that the island shall be acquired by the United States."

W. Louis Sonntag

236. As the possibility of American intervention in Cuba became more and more attractive to our diplomats, the government embarked on a great program of defensive armament. When the *Weekly* published this picture of the U. S. battleship *Indiana* on its trial run, the accompanying article characterized the navy as an "asylum for old age and a grave for youthful ambition."

Meanwhile the battle for newspaper circulation continued between Messrs. Pulitzer and Hearst, each trying to outdo the other in the manufacture of frightful tales of Spanish barbarity in Cuba. The chairman of the Senate's Foreign Relations Committee demanded (and got) recognition of Cuban belligerency with the aid of "evidence" of General Weyler's fiendish cruelty to the Cubans during the insurrection of 1868-1878, though it was easily demonstrable that Weyler hadn't even been in Cuba during those years. Senator Lodge was skillfully demonstrating that "Our immediate pecuniary interests in the island are very great." Even the *Weekly*, though admitting that "there is some doubt as to the truth" of the atrocity stories, lamented that "both insurgents and Spaniards are warring on the commerce of the United States."

William Allen Rogers

237. When Weyler finally adopted his plan of reconcentration, a plan which gathered all loyal Cubans into garrison towns and forbade the export of supplies to those who remained outside, he was merely reversing a tactic which had already been used by the Cuban General Gomez. But to the McKinley administration, which had just outwitted Bryan's "cross of gold" campaign in the 1896 election, the suffering which resulted from the reconcentration decree offered an acceptable diversion from domestic tribulations. Even the *Weekly*, one of the most conservative journals, fell for the propaganda and captioned this picture, "Starvation by Proclamation."

William Allen Rogers

238. The battleship *Maine* blew up in Havana Harbor on February 15, 1898, and no one thereafter really believed a war could be averted. Nobody had any evidence that the Spanish had destroyed the ship, nor has any such evidence been subsequently produced. "There is no cause for war," said the *Weekly*, and it launched a severe attack on "the noisy jingoes whose outcries are not inspired by patriotism, but by a desire for ignorant votes, or contracts for war supplies, or larger circulation, depending on the trade in which each particular jingo is engaged, whether it be politics or speculation or newspapers." But protests were useless. Recruits clustered about the army's offices, and Assistant Secretary Roosevelt was transforming the Navy Department from a "grave of youthful ambition" to a nursery of Presidents.

William Allen Rogers

239. The happy warrior being welcomed to Washington by this gay crowd of ladies and gentlemen is Consul-General Fitzburgh Lee. Lee had been appointed to Havana during Cleveland's administration and had distressed the Executive by his habit of "rolling intervention like a sweet morsel under his tongue." With bustling officiousness he continued, under McKinley, to magnify minor incidents into serious proportions, sending alarmist messages to Washington on the slightest provocation and thereby materially contributing to the ultimate conflict. He was, of course, rewarded with the plaudits of the populace and a commission as major-general in the army.

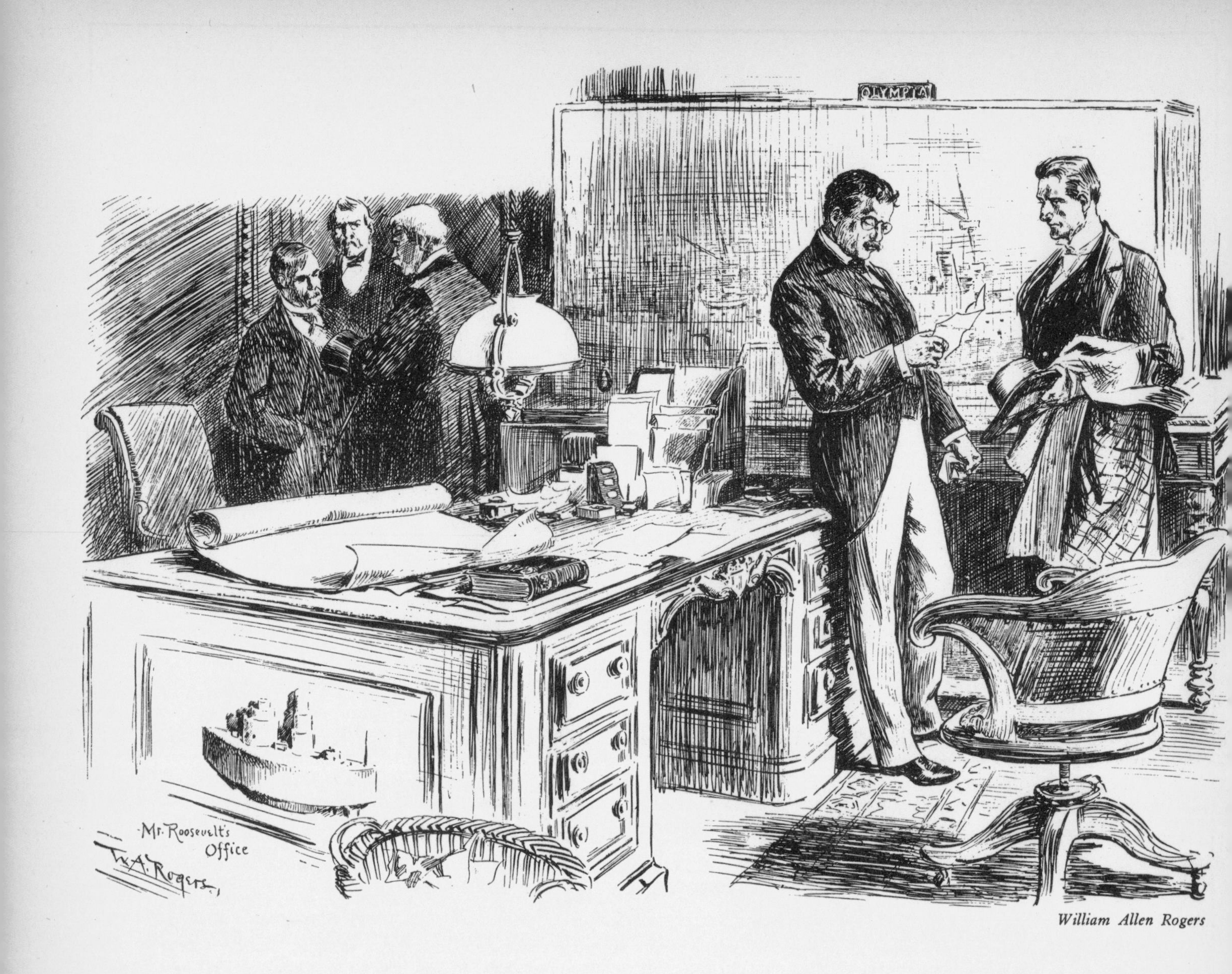

William Allen Rogers

240. So difficult had the problems of peace become that Secretary Long, of the navy, felt the need of a day's rest and went home early one Friday, leaving his assistant in charge. Senator Lodge just happened to drop in that afternoon, and he and his friend the Assistant Secretary discussed their old dream of acquiring the Philippine Islands. Without consulting Long or the President they began issuing orders, and it was thus that Commodore Dewey, out in the Pacific, got instructions that in the event of a declaration of war his duty would be to bottle up the Spanish Asiatic squadron and then commence "offensive operations in Philippine Islands."

John T. McCutcheon

241. Only in some cases were the news pictures in the *Weekly* drawn at the scene of action. They were often made by illustrators who had not witnessed the event, from sketches made on the spot by "special artists." This sketch, by John T. McCutcheon, was published without benefit of elaboration. It shows Mr. Wildman, U. S. consul at Hong Kong, waving good-by to Commodore Dewey as the *Olympia*, *Baltimore,* and *Rawleigh* sailed for Mirs Bay on April 25, 1898. Dewey had to leave Hong Kong in deference to Britain's neutrality, but he didn't want to sail for the Philippines until he had picked up some of the Aguinaldo insurrectionists to take with him. That was why he merely jogged his squadron over to Chinese territory at Mirs Bay. China, of course, was also a neutral, but, unlike Great Britain, had no army or navy to compel our recognition of her rights.

Harry Fenn

242. The battle of Manila Bay was the first important event of the war, and almost the only one which did not later become a scandal in the American press. Dewey's fleet completely destroyed the Spanish ships. Admiral Montojo had wisely decided to accept battle at anchor in the shallowest available water. There was one moment when things looks bad for our side; after two hours of what had appeared to be wholly ineffectual firing Dewey was informed that his flagship had only fifteen rounds of five-inch ammunition left. It was an embarrassing situation. He was seven thousand miles from a sure base of supplies, and as far as he could tell amid the clouds of smoke his notoriously inferior enemy was still intact. Fortunately it was all a mistake. There were more than fifteen rounds remaining. In fact only fifteen rounds had been fired. And, as the smoke of battle cleared, it was seen that most of the Spanish ships were already crippled.

Frederick Remington

243. Meanwhile the army had been having a tough time getting organized and the public demand for activity was becoming embarrassingly severe. It was decided, therefore, to send a shipment of arms to the Cubans with two companies of infantry as a guard. A side-wheeled river boat named the *Gussie* was accordingly dispatched on this secret enterprise. Secrecy was somewhat hampered by the presence of six newspaper reporters on board and of twenty-five other correspondents who followed in two tugs. It seemed as if everyone in Cuba knew the *Gussie* was coming, but she managed to land three Cuban guides without serious trouble. The guides couldn't find any insurgents, however, so the supplies were never landed and the *Gussie* paddled back to Florida.

Frederick Remington

244. One of the ablest and most abused commanders was Major-General William R. Shafter of the Fifth Army Corps. Faced with raw recruits, inadequate supplies, and a nightmare of jumbled transportation, he finally collected an expeditionary force at Tampa. Goaded to haste by a War Department which had no conception of his difficulties, heckled by public opinion which demanded action, and lampooned by the irrepressible Roosevelt, who had resigned from the Navy Department to join the Rough Riders, Shafter nevertheless managed to load most of his disorganized army onto transports. Then, just as he was laying down his seventh of a ton of weary flesh for a well-earned rest, word came from Washington that the army must not sail, after all. The navy wasn't sure where all the Spanish fleet was; so for another week the crowded troops sweltered at anchor before setting out for Santiago.

Carlton T. Chapman

245. While the army struggled desperately to put men in the field, the navy was capturing most of the newspaper headlines. Shortly after the magnificent news of Dewey's triumph at Manila, word came that Commodore Schley's Flying Squadron had bottled up the Spanish Atlantic fleet in Santiago Harbor. Actually Schley had been sent out to intercept Cervera's vessels before they reached port and had completely failed. His squadron had flown at seven knots, though it was capable of nearly twice that speed, and the foul-bottomed, out-classed Spanish ships had crossed the Atlantic, threaded the Carribbean, and sailed quietly in to the fortified protection of Santiago Harbor without even being sighted by an American vessel.

Thure de Thulstrup

246. Here is Captain Philip addressing his men on the *Texas* after the naval battle at Santiago. "I want to make public acknowledgment here," said the captain, "that I believe in God, the Father Almighty."

Cervera's fleet had tried to escape from the harbor by running our blockade. Admiral Sampson, who had joined Schley and taken command of the blockade, was unhappily not on hand at the supreme moment, having sailed off on his flagship to confer with the army leaders farther down the coast. But the Spanish vessels had old-fashioned wooden decks which caught fire easily, so that even though they pretty nearly did get away, a few well-aimed shots from our ships reduced them to howling infernos of flame. Then, while Captain Philip held divine service on his ship, Commodore Schley tactlessly signaled to the tardy Admiral, "We have gained a great victory. Details will be communicated," and was answered by a curt "Report your casualties." The seeds of bitter animosity had been planted, and the jealous commanders spent the rest of their lives in a bickering controversy. But for the moment people back home knew only that there had been another great victory.

J. A. Cahill

247. These flower-crowned soldiers are on their way from San Francisco to the Philippines. Their commanding officer is General Wesley Merritt, whom we met almost thirty years earlier at a West Point cadet hop (No. 17). On their way across the Pacific they will stop at the tiny island of Guam and be welcomed by the unsuspecting Spanish governor. They will inform him that they are not paying a courtesy visit, that war has broken out, and that they are annexing his island to the United States. Then they will sail on toward Manila.

T. DART. WALKER
GUAYAMA. P.R.
AUG 20-98

T. Dart Walker

248. Puerto Rico was also on the imperialist agenda, and Major-General Miles was hurriedly trying to conquer the island before the peace negotiations, which the Spanish government had already begun, could be completed. The conquest was not difficult. A newspaper correspondent named Stephen Crane captured one town all by himself—simply walked in, received the surrender, and waited for the troops to catch up with him.

The job was almost done when the end came. General Brooke had his army drawn up before Guayama on August 9th when a messenger came up to him bearing the President's peace message. "But three minutes and we should have fired," brooded the general.

Rufus Fairchild Zogbaum

249. In three months' time we had won the war, driven Spain from the Western Hemisphere, and acquired a considerable colonial empire. It was almost unbelievable.

The pleasurable excitement was dampened, however, by alarming reports of fever among the soldiers in Cuba. There were letters in the paper from Colonel Roosevelt telling of disastrous mismanagement and demanding that the troops be taken out of the plague-infested region. Soon transports were bearing the men to quarantine camp at Montauk, Long Island, and the epidemic was broken. Even so, disease killed almost eight hundred of the army—three times as many as were killed in battle.

Thure de Thulstrup

250. There was joy in the hearts of the Philippine insurgents when word came of Spain's defeat, and they organized a great triumphal parade through the streets of Manila. They naïvely believed that we had meant what we said about helping them to achieve independence. Scarcely any of them would have understood the implications of the *Weekly's* editorial attack on the "scheme for loading this country with the Philippines in the interest of what [President McKinley] calls 'destiny' and of what the missionaries call 'religion.'"

G. W. Peters

251. By February, 1899, the Philippine natives knew what we meant, and they began to fight for the freedom which we had encouraged them to expect. One of the most efficient commanders during the Philippine war was Colonel Frederick Funston, whose Twentieth Kansas Volunteers are here shown marching through the native village of Caloocan after having put its flimsy huts to the torch. Funston, who wanted to "rawhide these bullet-headed Asians until they yell for mercy" (*Weekly,* July 15, 1899, page 689), was soon promoted to a major-general's rank, and contributed heartily to the progress of our arms. But he was something of a pundit as well as a man of action. "After the war," he mused, "I want the job of Professor of American History in Luzon University, when they build it, and I'll warrant that the new generation of natives will know better than to get in the way of the bandwagon of Anglo-Saxon progress and decency."

W. T. Smedley

252. Early in the same year the S.S. *Paris* of the American Line carried four hundred and twenty passengers to Cuba for the first tourist invasion of the battlefields. This little group of pilgrims is inspecting the cell at Morro Castle where Lieutenant Hobson had been imprisoned. Hobson, of course, was the dashing young hero who had attempted to block the entrance to Santiago Harbor and thus prevent Cervera's exit. The plan had involved the grounding of the old collier *Merrimac* across the narrow channel, but had ended in failure. Hobson's exploit nevertheless was eagerly publicized by correspondents, and when the unfortunate lieutenant finally returned to his own country he was plagued by crowds of adoring women wherever he went.

William Allen Rogers

253. This picture of the New Orleans Sugar Exchange, drawn by W. A. Rogers in 1900, is an interesting sidelight on the imperial policy of the United States. The commodities listed on the bulletins include Puerto Rican molasses, sugar cane from Havana and Matanzas.

254. So popular had the horseless carriage become by 1900 that more than four thousand were manufactured in the year. The average price, computed from Census Bureau statistics, was in the neighborhood of $1,150, which is considerably less than it is popularly supposed to have been.

William Dodge Stevens

Although this W. D. Stevens drawing of "A Providential Encounter" shows a horse rescuing motorists who are out of gas, there were comparatively few gasoline cars on the road. Electrics and steamers dominated the highways for at least a decade.

William Allen Rogers

255. As the nineteenth century rolled majestically into its grave the politicians were eagerly plunging into another presidential contest. McKinley, up for re-election, flung "the full dinner-pail" slogan at his free-silver opponents and talked proudly of "the white man's burden" and our duty to uplift and Christianize the Philippines. Bryan, still fighting for free silver, advocated turning the islands over to the natives. McKinley and Roosevelt were backed by the industrial East, and this cartoon from the *Weekly* bluntly stresses the sectional character of the campaign. Bryan and a group of wild-eyed Western savages (including Debs) are represented as attacking the fortifications of the original thirteen states.

Uncle Sam defended the fort successfully; the Republicans won by a huge majority, and the newest of the earth's great nations had irrevocably shaped its course for thirty years.

INDEX

(Note: The numbers in this index do not refer to pages in the book, but to the numbered sections of the text. Names of artists and illustrators whose work is represented are printed in italics.)

Abbey, Edwin Austin, 110, 157
Abolitionists, 47, 48, 49, 83
Agrarian revolt, 160, 234
Agriculture, 32, 33, 36, 103, 104, 109, 160, 163, 221
Air-conditioned trains, 121
Airships, 40, 177
Alexandria Bay, 213
Ambulances, 178
American Peace Society, 54
Amusements, 5, 21-3, 27, 86, 87, 149-52, 158, 196, 209, 214, 218, 228
Anarchists, 201
Arc lamps, 174
Architecture, 127, 148, 204-7, 224, 225
Armstrong, M. K., 163
Art, 146, 147, 157, 190, 207, 224, 241
Arthur, Chester A., 196
Asbury Park, N. J., 212
Atlanta, Georgia, 185
Atlantic Cable, 39, 114
Automobiles, 254

Ballet, 27
Barnegat, 142
Barnum, P. T., 5, 86, 158
Barnum's Museum, 5
Barnwell, Robert W., House of, 81
Baseball, 24
Bathing, 18, 149, 214
Bayonet fighting in Civil War, 65
Beaufort, N. C., 81
Bell, Alexander Graham, 179
Belmont, August, 19
Bergh, Henry, 141
Bessemer converters, 188
Bicycle Clubs, 216
Booth's accomplices, Execution of, 100
Boston, 6, 22, 49, 123
Boston Common, 22
Bridgeport, Conn., 186
Bradley, Horace, 185

Broadway, N. Y., 5, 54
Brodie, Steve, 199
"Brooklyn," sloop of war, 61
Brooklyn Bridge, 207
Brotherhood of Locomotive Engineers, 197
Brown, John, 8, 48
Buchanan, James, 45
Buffalo, Herds of, 167
Bush, C. G., 151, 159
Butterfield's Overland Mail, 42, 161

Cahill, J. A., 247
Camp, Walter, 228
Camp meetings, 143
Carnegie's steel works, 188
Carpet-baggers, 106, 107, 109
Castle Garden, N. Y., 3
Cattle industry, 164-6, 219, 220
"Cattle Queen," 220
Centennial Exhibition, 169-72
Central Park, N. Y., 23
Chapman, Carlton T., 245
Chicago, 34, 119, 200, 224-6, 233
Chinese labor, 116
Church, Frederick Stuart, 156
Cimmaron, Colorado, 220
Cincinnati, 35, 36
Circus, 158
Civil Service reform, 196
Civil War: Confederate Army, 57, 64, 67, 69, 73, 76; Confederate Navy, 63; diplomacy during, 84, 85; discipline, 69, 70; mobilization, 53-8, prisoners, 75; propaganda, 67; supplies, 58; surgery, 68; tactics, 65-7, 72, 97, 98; Union Army, 53-6, 58, 96, 97; Union Navy, 61, 62, 95
Clemens, Samuel L., *see* Mark Twain
Coaching, 217
Cold Spring, N. Y., 60
Colorado, 210, 219, 220
Columbia College Crew, 153
Commonwealth Ave., Boston, 123

Communists, 200, 201
Concord, N. H., 7
Coney Island, 149, 214
Confederacy, The, 51ff, 103
Construction train, 120
Corruption, 80, 96, 107, 131, 132, 137-40, 195
Cowboys, 164, 219
Coxey's Army, 232
Cozzen's Hotel, West Point, 17
Cozzens, Frederick Swartwout, 182
Crane, Stephen, 248
Crew Races, 153
Crime, 133, 203
Croquet, 151
Cuba, 46, 135, 235ff
Cuban Insurrectionists, N. Y. office of, 135

Dancing, 17, 228
Darwinism, 211
Davidson, J. O., 174, 181
Davis, Jefferson, 10, 51, 103
Davis, Theodore R., 57, 63, 72, 106, 113, 135, 143, 153, 161, 167, 169, 170, 186
Day, Ben, Jr., 149
Day, Clarence, Sr., 230
Debs, Eugene, 233
Depressions, 28, 133, 226, 232
Dewey, George, 241, 242
Dickens, Charles, 145
Dielman, Frederick, 112
Diplomacy, 45, 46, 84, 253ff
Domestic servants, 14
Draft Riots, 94
Dubuque, Iowa, 56

East St. Louis, 199
Edison, Thomas A., 173, 176
Education, 25, 154, 155
Electricity, 173, 174, 179
Electric train, 173
Elevated railroad, 124, 192
Emerson, Ralph W., 49, 100
Ericsson, John, 62

Expansion of cities, 1, 36, 123, 124, 127, 192, 222
Exports, 191
Eytinge, Sol, 74, 211

Factories, 7, 30, 59, 115, 186
Fashions, 12, 13, 18, 19, 30, 80, 91, 150, 213, 215, 228, 231
Feminists, 231
Fenn, Harry, 242
Fielden, Samuel, 200
Finance, 29, 93, 126, 131, 132, 192, 230, 253
Financial panics, 27, 28, 133, 194
Findlay, Ohio, 175
Fire Departments, 136
Fishing, 196
Fisk, James, 126, 131
Fiske, John, 211
Flood, James C., House of, 205
Flying Squadron, The, 245
Football, 25
Forbes, Edwin, 33
Fort Sumter, 52
Fox Hunting, 218
Fox, Stanley, 122, 124, 125, 129, 134, 139
Fredericks, Alfred, 14, 45
Freight Handlers Union, 198
Freight rates, 188, 189
Frenzeny and Tavernier, 117, 158, 162, 164, 165, 166
Frost, Arthur Burdett, 229
Funston, Frederick, 251

Galena, Illinois, 111
Gallagher's night stock exchange, 93
Garfield, James A., 179, 184
Garrison, William Lloyd, 49
Geological Survey, 210
Georgia, 97
Gold mining, 43
Goldman, Emma, 201
Golf, 229
Gordon, Nathaniel, Hanging of, 83
Gould, Jay, 131, 132
Graham, Charles, 175, 187, 188, 193, 203, 209, 220, 224
Grand Central Depot, N. Y., 122, 192
Grangers, 160
Grant, Ulysses S., 71, 72, 111, 148, 170, 194, 195
Grant & Ward, Failure of, 194
Grant's tomb, 195
"Great Eastern," 38
Gribayedoff, V., 201
"Gussie" expedition, 243

Hamilton, J. R., 102, 103
Harper's Ferry, 48
Harvard College, 25; crew, 153
Hassam, Childe, 235
Havana, 235
Hayden Survey, 210
Haymarket Riot, 200
Hell's Kitchen, 203
Hennessy, William John, 2
Herman, Mr. (of St. Paul), 85
Higginson, Thomas W., 23
Hitchcock, 1
Hoboken, N. J., 21, 24, 183
Hobson, R. P., 252
Hog slaughtering, 35
Homer Winslow, 6, 17, 18, 21-3, 25, 26, 59, 65, 66, 77, 115, 133, 150, 155
Homestead Act, 163
Homestead Strike, 201
Hoop Skirts, 12, 13, 30
Hoppin, Augustus, 19, 20, 46
Horse racing, 26, 150
Hunt, R. M., 204

Illinois Central R. R., 34, 89
Immigrants, 2, 3, 7, 116, 134, 135
Imperialism, 46, 135, 235ff
"Indiana," U.S.S., 236
Indians, 85, 120, 161, 223
Industrial fairs, 185, 187
Industry, 30, 31, 34-6, 89, 91, 92, 95, 102, 109, 110, 119, 164, 173, 182, 184-7, 191, 232, 233
Inventions, 32, 40, 173-81, 191

Jackson, "Stonewall," 76
James River Canal, 57, 102
Japanese Ambassadors, First, 45
Johnson, Andrew, 101, 112, 113
Journalism, 44, 113, 156, 201, 243
Joutel, Louis, 206

Kane, Delancey, 217
Keetels, C. A., 176
King, Clarence, 210
Ku Klux Klan, 108

Labor, 30, 59, 83, 94, 115-8, 120, 129, 197-201, 226, 232, 233
"Lady Davis," armed steamer, 63
Land Grants, 90, 163
Laver & Curlett, architects, 205
Lawrence, Mass., 115
Lecompton, Kansas, 8
Lee, Fitzhugh, 239
Lee, Robert E., 48, 73, 98, 100
Leisser, M. B., 197
Lewis, Robert, 118
Libby Prison, 75
Life-Saving Service, U. S., 142
Lighting, 174, 175, 182
Lincoln, Abraham, 37, 50
Lincoln, Mrs. Abraham, 79
Lindell Hotel, St. Louis, 90
Literature, 74, 145, 146, 208
Livry, Emma, 27
Lodge, Henry Cabot, 236, 240
Long Branch, N. J., 148
Longworth, Nicholas, House of, 36
Lowe, Carlincourt, 40
Lumbering, 31
Lynching, 47

M'Callum, A., 100
McCutcheon, John T., 241
McKinley, William, 225, 227
Machinery, 30, 32, 170, 171, 173
Maddaus, O. W., 147
Mail-order houses, 159
Maine, 31
Manila, P. I., 250
Manila Bay, Battle of, 242
Manufacturing, 30, 59, 60, 64, 91, 115, 186, 188
Mark Twain, 41, 195, 208
Meat-packing, 119, 191
Meeker, E., 178
Memphis, 96
Menlo Park, California, 205
Menlo Park, N. J., 173
Mente, Charles, 226
Mercer, Asa S., 168
Merchants, 28, 49, 91, 127, 159
Merrill, F. T., 231
Merritt, Wesley, 17, 247
"Meteor," first mastless steamship, 181
Millandon plantation, 109
Mississippi, 10
Mississippi, Navigation on the, 41
"Molly Maguires," 117

Monopoly, 114
Montgomery, Ala., 51
Morgan, John, 67
Morro Castle, 252
Morton, Oliver P., 112
Moving Day, 14
Mulberry St. tenement, 128
Music, 146, 180

Nadherny, E. V., 230
Nast, Thomas, 54, 67, 68, 87, 116, 137, 138, 140, 160, 184, 189, 208
Natural gas, 175
Negroes, 81, 82, 94, 101, 103, 104, 107
Nevin, M., 38
New Bedford, 182
New Haven, 288
New Orleans, 105, 109; 253
New York Central R. R., 122, 198
New York City, 1, 3-5, 14, 21, 23, 26, 28, 29, 38, 50, 54, 93-5, 114, 122, 124, 126-9, 132-4, 139, 191, 192, 194, 195, 198, 202-4, 207, 209, 217, 227, 230, 238
Newport, R. I., 18, 19
Newspapers, 58, 113, 137, 139, 156, 171, 201, 222, 243
Nichols, Henry Hobart, 227
Nyack, N. Y., 181

Ocean Grove, N. J., 212
Oil, 92
Oklahoma, 223
Ostentation, 19, 79, 80, 127, 205
Oxen, 33
Oyster Bay, L. I., 218

"Pacific," sidewheeler, 41
Paris, Count of, 29
Parks, 22, 23
"Passaic," ironclad, 62
Peddlers, 159
Pennell, Joseph, 190
Pennsylvania coal region, 117
Pennsylvania Station, Philadelphia, 190
Perkins, Granville, 142
Pershing, John J., 199
Peters, G. W., 251
Philadelphia, 169, 190, 216
Philip, Captain, of the "Texas," 246
Philippine Islands, 250, 251
Phonograph, 176
Photography, 157
Picnics, 21, 149
Pike's Peak gold region, 43
Pittsburgh, 187, 197
Plantations, Southern, 10, 109
Politics, 50, 105-7, 112-4, 139, 189, 234, 237, 255
Populists, 234
Portland, Maine, 44
Poverty, 4, 128, 129, 202, 203, 226, 227
Pranishnikoff, I. P., 191, 210
Prince of Wales, 44
Profiteers, 80, 95
Prospectors, 162
Public health, 4, 128, 179
Puerto Rico, 248
Pullman Palace Hotel Car, 121
Pullman Strike, 233

Quick-lunch counter, 130
Quincy, Mass., 206

Radical Republicans, 100, 105, 107, 109, 112, 113
Railroads, 34, 88, 89, 103, 112, 120-2, 173, 189, 190, 197, 198
Ramseur, Stephen D., 17
Read, Thomas Buchanan, 74
Ready-made clothing, 91
Reapers, Machine, 32
Reconstruction, 100-10, 112, 113
Recruiting (1898), 238
Refrigeration, 191
Reinhart, Charles Stanley, 130, 141, 144
Religion, 143, 211, 212
Remington, Frederick, 223, 233, 243, 244
Richardson, Henry H., 206
Richmond, Va., 64, 75, 98, 102, 103
"River Queen," steam yacht, 152
Rix, Julian W., 195
Rockefeller, John D., 189
Rocky Mountains, 162
Roeblings, The, father and son, 207
Rogers, William Allen, 183, 202, 214, 219, 232, 237-40, 253, 255
Roosevelt, Theodore, 218, 219, 240
Ruffin, Edmund, 52, 99
St. Andrews Golf Club, 229
St. Augustine, Fla., 215
St. Louis, 90
Salt Lake City, 9
San Francisco, 42, 247
Saratoga, 150, 153
Savannah, 174
Saxophone, 180
Schell & Hogan, 171, 194
Schley, W. S., 245
"School for Scandal," 209
Schools, 155
Schwab's, Justus, saloon,
Science, 210, 211
Sentiment, 146
Seventh Regiment, 54
Seward, William H., 84
Shafter, William R., 244
Shantyville, at Centennial, 172
Sharpshooter, 66
Sheppard, W. L., 104, 107
Sheridan, Phil., 74
Sherman's March to the Sea, 97
Shinkle, W., 179
Shipping, 126, 191
Ships, 38, 41, 61, 63, 95, 126, 181, 182, 191, 236, 245
Shockoe Creek Valley, 103
Simplot, Alexander, 96
Sing-Sing village, 143
Skating, 23, 87
Slabtown, Va., 101
Slavery, 81-3
Slums, 4, 128, 202, 203
Smedley, W. T., 213, 252
Smith, F. Hopkinson, 207
Snyder, W. P., 192, 221, 228
S.P.C.A., 141
Sonntag, W. Louis, 236
South Dakota, 234
Spanish-American War: Army, 238, 243, 244, 247, 248; diplomacy, 239; disease, 249; Navy, 236, 240, 241, 242, 245, 246; propaganda, 237
Sports, 18, 22-6, 87, 150-3, 196, 216-8, 229
Springfield, Ill., 37
Stevens, Thaddeus, 100, 112
Stevens, William Dodge, 254
Stewart, A. T., House of, 127
Stock Exchange, 93, 193, 230
Stock Yards, Chicago, 119
"Stonington," sidewheeler, 126

Stout, A. V., House of, 15
Strikes, 94, 117, 197-201, 233
Stuart, J. E. B., 73
Sub-Treasury, N. Y., 29
Suburban life, 15, 192, 205
Subway, 125
Sugar-cane mill, 109
Surgery, 179
Syracuse, 32

Tammany Ring, 131, 137-40
"Tantivy," 217
Tarrytown, N. Y., 15
Taylor, Frank Hamilton, 215
Taylor Hotel, Jersey City, 131
Telegraph, 39, 58, 114
Temperance, 144
Tenements, 4, 128, 203
Texas, 166
"Texas," battleship, 246
Thayer, Russell, 177
Theater, 27, 209
Thulstrup, Thure de, 199, 200, 225, 246, 250
Titusville, Penna., 92
Tom Thumb, General, 86
Topeka, Kansas, 221
Transportation, 16, 20, 34, 38, 40-2, 57, 88, 102, 112, 120-2, 124, 125, 161, 181, 190, 216, 254
Tredegar Iron Works, 64
Trenton Falls, 84
"Trilby," 231
Turpentine distillery, 110
Tweed, William M., 131, 137-40

Union League Clubs, 107
Union Pacific R.R., 120, 121
Unions, 118, 197-9, 233

Vacations, 16-8, 20, 21, 84, 148, 149, 212-5
Vanderbilt, W. K., House of, 204
Vanderhoof, C. A., 128
Vassar College, 154
Vermilion, Dakota Territory, 163
Vicksburg, 72
Vigilantes, 166
Vizetelly, Henry, 76

Wages, 14, 30, 115, 118
Walker, T. Dart, 248
Wall Street, 132, 194
Wallace, Lew, 70
Wallack's Theater, 209
Warren, A. W., 98
Warren, Lavinia, 86
Washington, D. C., 11, 78, 112, 113, 239, 240
Washington St., Boston, 6
Washington Territory, University, 168
Watertown, Mass., 59
Waud, A. R., 3, 10, 73, 78, 105, 109, 120, 121, 126
Waud, W., 131
Webb's Shipyard, 95
Weldon, C. D., 198
Wesleyan Univ. Crew, 153
West Point, 17
West Point Foundry, 60
Whalers, 182
White Mountains, 20
Whitman, Walt, 172
Wichita, Kansas, 165, 222
Wilson, Thomas and Catherine, 203
Wilson's Zouaves, 55
Women, 12, 28, 30, 77, 78, 80, 118, 155, 168, 220, 228, 231
Women's Protective Assn., 118
World's Fair, Chicago, 224, 225
Worrall, H., 217
Worth, Thomas, 28
Wrigley, Capt. Harry E., of Topographical Engineers, 75

Xenia, Ohio, 144

Yachting, 152, 215
Yale University crew, 228
Yonkers, N. Y., 229
Young, Brigham, 9

Zogbaum, Rufus Fairchild, 249
"Zum Groben Michel," 201